TATA'S TREE

A Memoir of Life in the Back of the Yards

TATA'S TREE

A Memoir of Life in the Back of the Yards

by

Pat Carpenter-Wood

1stBooks – rev. 5/31/00

ABOUT THE BOOK

Memories of an era past…of a neighborhood that no longer exists. A time when sidewalks and gutters were swept clean each morning and burning autumn leaves evoked thoughts of baked potatoes.

Hot summer evenings were spent outdoors visiting with neighbors while children played hide and seek or chased fireflies. The first winter snow fall meant sledding down a viaduct grading or ice-skating across the lagoon in Sherman Park.

Memories of the changes that slowly changed a neighborhood, and how one family coped with new beginnings. "Tata's Tree' was written not only as a reminder of the legacy and the deep roots left by those beginnings, but it is also meant to be an inspiration to a new generation of immigrants and their family that each day should be met with that renewal of hope.

The sketches in this book were drawn mostly from memory, the authors and her elders. The passage of time may have repainted some events and places to the slight injury of accuracy.

Some historical information was obtained from the following books:

Polish Immigrants and Industrial Chicago, Dominic A. Pacyga

Nature's Metropolis, Chicago and the Great West, William Cronon

Everyday Life from Prohibition through World War II, Marc McCutcheon

*Written in loving memory of my father, Leon Kalinowski, and
my mother, Henrietta Kalinowski, (Henryka Gajeck)*

FORWARD

In 1971, when I left Chicago and moved to Tucson with my first husband Jim, I did so rather reluctantly. I felt deeply that I was abandoning my oldest son, his wife and the wonderful grandchildren they gave me; plus a daughter in college and a middle son who was still trying desperately to find his way in life. Most of all, I was not only leaving behind a beloved city where I was born and raised, I was also leaving the two people who had taught me the virtues of strength and fortitude, and how life must go on despite changes. And so, with Nancy and Tom, my youngest children, and with the hope of reconciling a marriage and the love of a husband, I moved to Tucson.

Unfortunately, illness stepped into my marriage before its fragile existence could find enough strength and love to heal itself. Weekly letters and an occasional phone call to family back home kept my spirit alive...without these I may have become totally oblivious to what I left behind.

For the next eight years I became lost in the dusky world of nursing an ill husband and a loveless marriage. My unrequited skills ended when Jim died in the winter of 1980. And by that summer, although I found a special love for this new city, and relished the quiet beauty of its desert scene, I felt empty inside and in dire need of visiting the home and family I left in the Midwest.

This first visit after an absence of eight years was joyful. To see my oldest son Tim and his family greatly unburdened my heavy heart. Even Jim, my middle son, seemed untouched by the distance that existed between us for so long. But it was finally being with my father and mother again that renewed my strength and courage to get on with my life and find new meaning in myself.

My parents were still living in the same neighborhood and the same house where I was born and raised. In those eight years nothing much had changed. I felt like a child again, asking to be nurtured by their love and joy. With renewed determination, I returned to Tucson to continue my life.

I had forgotten how quickly those things we hope might remain untouched by time and circumstance can actually change within a blink of an eye. When I was summoned back to Chicago in 1981 it was because my mother suddenly took ill. Staying with my father while my mother was confined in hospital, I realized now how much this familiar place had changed.

Families from the past were gone; the homes that once were kept neat and tidy, now belonged to absentee landlords and were left rather forsaken to tenants who, for the sake of argument, had better things to think about then caring for this property they called home. I began to think it would be wise for my mother and father to sell this home and move back to Tucson with me.

My father thought the idea not only absurd, also sinful. To leave the home he had brought his bride to so many years back and cared for with love was an outlandish idea. When Mama recovered from her illness and returned home, she totally agreed with him. So once again, with less hope this time that all would remain the same, I returned to Tucson. Life for me as about to change as well, when I married a delightfully loving man in 1982. I took my new husband, Frank, back to Chicago with me in hopes my family would accept him into their life. They did, with open arms. When we returned to Tucson, I found new faith that life at last was almost perfect.

But later that year, I was called once again to Chicago. This time my father had taken ill. And this time I knew it was something my mother could not handle all by herself. Cancer of the bladder would render my father almost completely bed-ridden, and my mother was now bent so badly with osteoporosis that the idea of moving them to Tucson was no longer a shocking suggestion.

Although my sister Halina and her family lived in Chicago, they still had children living at home. The possibility of caring for two older parents was, at most, difficult…the probability that my sister would eventually have to take them into her home seemed, at this time, out of the question. So I finally succeeded into talking both my father and mother into selling their home and moving in with me. So once again, my Mama and Tata became a part of my life.

As in the past, Tata accepted this change in his life with great aplomb. And Mama—she told me often how grateful she was that she had someone with her every day to help with the struggle of caring for my father and for the chance to be with her daughter again.

Tata especially loved the trees around our home. He marveled at the fact on how little watering our Palo Verde trees needed. He remembered the daily watering of that tree in front of our home back in Chicago, on Loomis Street, and how proud he always was of its growth and strength.

Tata died a peaceful death in his own bed in 1987. He was ninety-six years old. He looked seventy.

Mama died one year later. She was eighty-five. Her struggle to continue on with life had made her weary and bed ridden toward the end. So suddenly, the emptiness that entered my life again could not even be filled by a loving husband or my happy marriage. Perhaps if I returned to my roots, to that home and neighborhood where I had learned that life had to go on despite changes and regardless of what fate ordained for us, I would heal.

So in 1990 I returned again to Chicago. This trip was not so much to visit with family; by now a family reunion had brought them to Tucson the year before Mama's death. I returned to the city of my youth to visit the past and to remember what Tata and Mama taught me: that life must go on.

For years I carried a picture in my mind of that last day, how Loomis Street and our home looked when Mama and Tata said good-bye to Chicago. Like a picture hanging on a wall, that image never changed. I never imagined how fiercely cruel and damaging real life could be. And like a thief, reality tried to steal away my picture and memories.

A street once swept clean every morning by immigrants who were determined to find a better way of life was now covered with the litter of lives undeniably festering away in apathy. Homes once showered with a fresh coat of paint and dressed in constant repair, were now shameful in a dress of peeling paint and obvious disrepair. Windows, once proud and bright with weekly washing, were dusty with dirt or worse, gaping empty holes that seemed to scream out for bygone days.

Most of the homes on my street, 49th. and Loomis, were gone—either burned down or crumbled away. The home where I was born and raised, although still standing, was a mute reminder of what this neighborhood once was. The little green bench Tata built for us still sat in place. Unpainted and wobbly now, it brought back cheerful memories of a place now gloomy with neglect. But best of all, his tree was there—still tall, still sturdy, the leaves still green, reigning like a stately monarch, perhaps observing what his kingdom had now become. It was the sight of this tree that gave me solace and reminded me of what Tata once said: our good memories are what help us continue with life…despite changes, despite ordeals. Like his tree, we had to stay strong and sturdy and somehow continue on.

It was when my oldest son Tim visited that same neighborhood in 1997 that I knew I had to write the story of those days and all I could remember of what once used to be. When Tim phoned me and told me what 49th. and Loomis had become, I was terribly thankful I had not seen the continued ruins with my own eyes.

The only house standing on this street now was the one numbered 4936; my home—Tata and Mama's home. When I talked of my sadness with Claudia and Nancy, my daughters, they encouraged me to write about a time and neighborhood from a forgotten past. As I began this story for them, and for my grandchildren and great-grandchildren, I wanted them to realize that a part of their heritage was not this festering forgotten neighborhood. This was not what their ancestors found and nurtured when they moved on this street. More, I wanted them to feel what Tata felt when he nurtured the tree that grew so tall and strong, and to know that despite all obstacles, we must do our best to make life worthwhile. That the nurturing of that belief can only come from us. Now I feel this story will not only reach their hearts, but the hearts of many others as well. Especially those who find life a constant struggle.

POLAND, THE CITY OF CZESTOHOWA

From 1795 to 1918, the Poles, although a nation, were without a country. Their kingdom was divided in three parts, their armies were dispersed. In some places even their mother language was forbidden, especially in public schools. It was for this very reason that one particular mother and father decided to find a country that would be more suitable for raising their two daughters.

The country they chose was America. That mother would one day be my grandmother. I never knew her first name. To me she would always be known as Babsha, which means Grandmother in Polish. So in the following story, when I speak of Babsha, you will know I refer to my grandmother.

Babsha's two daughters were named Izabella, (my aunt), and Henryka, (my mother). My story begins with their decision to make that journey to America.

AMERICA

I would never meet my grandfather. In 1912, when this family, whose surname was Gajeck, decided to migrate to America, this husband and father knew that his wife and two daughters would have to make the journey without him.

I do know when my grandfather married my grandmother he held a teaching position in a small private boys school. Since my grandmother was a midwife in Poland, this was a family that lived quite comfortably until my grandfather became ill with consumption.

About this same time the country of Poland was in turmoil and the new barriers of forbidding the use of their Polish language in school convinced my grandparents that they must seek freedom elsewhere. But the decision would be a bittersweet one. Although it meant great educational freedom for their daughters, it also meant a breaking up of this close and loving family.

Perhaps from stories she heard, or letters Babsha received from her brother, my uncle, Wujeck Janek, who lived in America, my grandparents knew that the immigration authorities would never allow my grandfather's entry into America...not with consumption. So it must have been with a great amount of sadness and a very heavy heart that this young mother and her two children set out alone for a country and land they only knew about from what Babsha's brother revealed in his letters.

Their good-byes on that last day in Poland most certainly were tearful. Mama often told me how Babsha cried as she held on to her tall and handsome husband for what may have been the very last time. To think she might never see him again surely broke her heart. If she had known that he would die three months later, would they have made the trip? A question I once asked Mama. 'His death,' she replied,' came so soon after because of loneliness. No doubt his heart was broken on that day of our departure.'

But Mama knew, long before Babsha received news of her darling husband's death, that the man they would never see again had left them forever.

More then once Mama told the story of that evening when sitting on her mother's lap, resting her head against a warm bosom as Babsha sang a Polish lullaby, of the image that came to her in the kitchen doorway. Mama sat facing that doorway, her sleepy eyes slowly closing, when out of nowhere an image appeared in that doorway. Mama was wide awake now as she gazed at the shadowy figure.

At first the figure was unrecognizable, but soon it became clearer to her. Mama could clearly see it was her darling father. She stretched out her arm and pointed, whispering the word, 'Tatush', which is an endearing Polish version of 'darling father'. Babsha, perhaps thinking the child was merely expressing desire to see her father, ignored the gesture. When Mama repeated the word, Babsha finally stopped singing and asked her little daughter what was wrong. Before Mama could explain, the figure vanished. Mama always believed it was at that very moment her father died. When a letter finally arrived from a dear neighbor in Poland, notifying Babsha of her husband's death, the date on that letter corresponded with the day Mama saw the image.

Babsha was, without any doubt, a woman of unbelievable courage. To leave ones husband and country and travel that distance to an unknown place with two small children in hand was not an unknown act of valor to many other women migrating to America. To maintain a stable and living life once arriving to this country took more then courage. It took an inner boldness and strength not known to fainthearted women. And when Mama recounted their journey across the Atlantic to me, I knew Babsha was one who had that undaunted spirit.

'We came to America by steerage, on a big steamship. It was very dark in that hole.' Mama of course meant the 'hold'; to her it was clearly a dark, black hole. 'The smell was awful. This room was packed with men, women and children. Each family was given a pot for bodily waste; one that was emptied only every other day. By the time our journey ended, the stench was almost unbearable. Perhaps others felt as I did, if we could bear this, we would be rewarded well in our new country.

'More children then adults became sick with vomiting and diarrhea. They cried almost constantly during this journey of twelve…perhaps thirteen days. True, not many days, yet it seemed a lifetime to me. I was only nine years old at the time. Izabella was two years older.'

Mama said that Babsha urged both of them to sleep as much as they could 'It will make the journey pass more quickly.' Babsha said.

'But', Mama always added in her stories, 'I think she wanted us to sleep so we would not hear her quiet sobbing, which mostly came at night. During the day she tried to stay cheerful.'

Before leaving their home in Poland, Babsha boiled some eggs and potatoes. This, with a small loaf of bread, and a jar of water supplied by the crew of the boat, helped sustain them during their journey. Mama said she looked forward to mornings aboard the vessel. It was then the door above the hold was opened to allow a bit of fresh air down to the passengers below. Best of all, the travelers on deck would throw oranges and nuts down to the immigrants below. Everyone scrambled for those treats, even Babsha. Once, when Tata took all of us to the zoo, during one of our Sunday excursions, I laughed at the monkeys as they hurried to grab the food we tossed at them. Mama did not. As we walked away she said: 'perhaps that is what we looked like in that hole, and why the people above laughed at us.' I could only think how sad for those immigrants; yet what strength it took to obliterate such feelings and thoughts.

The possessions the Gajeck family carried with them were minimal. One large satchel that held Babsha's feather quilt, a few doilies crochet by her mother, and a small print of the Blessed Lady of Czestochowa. Izabella carried a smaller satchel that held two changes of clothing for each of them. Mama was put in charge of a still smaller bundle which held their food. Both girls stayed close to their mother at all times. Mama and Babsha slept with their head against the large satchel, while Izabella rested on hers.

'The ocean stayed calm for most of that journey.' Mama told me as she talked about her trip. 'Only once did I become sick from the boats rocking motion. My mother put cool compresses on my forehead. They helped a bit, at least enough to help me sleep better.'

Perhaps this was the reason Mama always refused to try any rides at White City Amusement park. She also hated when Tata insisted on driving his car along the trolley track, which made the vehicle sway a bit. The memory of that seasickness stayed imbedded in her mind forever.

But soon their terrifying journey was coming to an end. Another soon to begin.

ELLIS ISLAND AND A NEW WORLD

'Suddenly everyone was being herded on to a smaller boat. The confusion was mind-boggling.' Mama said as she reiterated that last day of their journey. My Mama quickly gathered up her satchel and told both of us to hang close to her side.' As Mama spoke I could only imagine how bewildered and frightened this little group of three must have been as they were whisked away to a smaller boat that would carry them to Ellis Island.

Mama remembered that day quite well. How all the immigrants were lined up to be examined by a stranger in a strange uniform. Their eyes, nose and chest...all had to be in perfect order to pass entry into their new country. But this was not as terrifying as the fact that they were separated from each other during this spell of inspection. Mama said all she could do is wonder if she would ever see her Mama and sister again.

Surprisingly, there she was, waiting for her two daughters. At last they were together again. Now they were led to yet another room. A large room filled with tables and benches and a high ceiling covered with a huge American flag. They were seated at one of the tables and beneath the flag of their new country were fed soup and bread. It was during this feast the Gajeck family had their first taste of fruit called banana.

'It felt so good to have my belly full again. Afterwards I wished I could lay down someplace and take a nap. But it could not be. Soon we were all escorted to a table where our names were about to be changed.'

The Gajeck family was luckier perhaps then most. Some immigrants not only had their given name changed, but the family name as well. In Mama's case her given name was changed from Henryka to Henrietta; Izabella became Isabelle. With that done, the next stop came at the money exchange booth. The Polish money they carried, called Zloty, was exchanged for American money.

'Everything happened so quickly.' Mama continued as she recounted that day. 'I thought it a miracle that soon we would step upon the land that would be our new home. I was so tired I hardly noticed what the city of New York looked like at this time. Mama also seemed only anxious to get on a train that would take us to Chicago.'

How they managed to find the right train in this strange city Mama never fully explained. They spoke no English, so it stands to reason they may have found someone that spoke both Polish and English who gave them directions to the train station. Nonetheless, soon they were aboard that train and on their way to Chicago. Wujeck Janek, the Polish derivative of Uncle John, would be waiting for their arrival.

From everything he had written to them about this great new country I am sure Babsha had high hopes of finding a decent job and earning a decent enough wage to care for her family. After all, she was fairly well educated and a midwife in Poland. Surely a position in this field would be easily found. As to their living quarters, Babsha's brother had assured her she would be comfortable.

Unfortunately, her first hopes were shattered quickly after only a few weeks time. Being a woman and with the Polish language her only means of communication, Babsha had two strikes against her as soon as she stepped upon Ellis Island. Being a woman in her middle thirties, with two small children to care for without a husband, was the third strike that sealed her fate. For now, until she found other employment, Babsha would have to rely on her brother's help.

Uncle Janek was a dapper looking man. Although short in stature, about five foot six to be exact, he carried himself well. With his neatly waxed mustache, a trimmed short thick beard, he looked rather debonair. His black hair matched eyes as black as bitter chocolate drops, Uncle Janek was always immaculate in dress and appearance. Mama claimed he migrated to America for only one reason: to find a wealthy woman and marry her. For now, on the day he met his sister and two nieces, he was still single. He worked as a tool and die maker in a factory on Chicago's north side. His living quarters were on the south side of the city.

'That day was hot and humid. ' Mama continued her story. 'Sweat poured down my back like a small stream of water. The wool dress I wore stuck to my skin like glue. The wool stockings I wore felt so uncomfortable and my legs felt so weak. Whether that was from the long trip or the heat I did not know. When Uncle Janek embraced my Mama and then knelt down beside Isabelle and me he pulled us close to him. Suddenly all was well. I felt such great relief that he was there beside us.

Janek took each girl by their hand and chattering away with his sister, who, Mama said, looked happy for the first time since boarding the boat, led them to his waiting horse and buggy outdoors.

Riding in Uncle Janek's buggy that first day rendered Babsha speechless. 'No doubt this city of tall buildings dumbfounded her. But I am sure it was more the congestion of people and buggies, electric streetcars, horse carts, and so much noise, that frightened and overwhelmed her,' Mama told me. 'Isabelle and I clung tightly to Uncle Janek's hand. The thought of getting lost in this crowd frightened me.'

Of course, none of the three new arrivals knew they were being introduced to Chicago's business district. It would probably be much later that Babsha realized this was a far better sight then the one awaiting them on Chicago's south side. That area where Uncle Janek lived was far removed from the palatial homes they witnessed on this first ride through downtown Chicago. A new home so much different from their cozy home in Poland.

THE STOCKYARD DISTRICT

Uncle Janek arrived in Chicago in 1889. He found his way to Chicago and this district on the simple advice of friends who were already living in Chicago and working in the stockyards.

Originally the meat packing and steel industries were located closer to Chicago's business district. When the Union Stockyard opened in 1865, the start of Chicago's south side manufacturing district began.

Work on the new livestock market began on June seventh. Plans included construction of pens to hold cattle, hogs, sheep and horses. Surrounded by railroad tracks, the location included a hotel, a restaurant, and later a post office and bank. In this self-contained unit, plans to build housing for an expected increase in workers, also became part of the plan. By 1900 the original 320 acres increased to 475 acres. The stockyards and packing houses now employed 32,000 people. And Uncle Janek, who was a tool and die maker by trade, had to take his first job here.

This job helped pay his rent and put food on the table. One year later, with a fair knowledge of English, and with a friends help, Janek fell into a job on the north side of Chicago that allowed him to follow his trade. Staying on in his living quarters on the south side puzzled Mama even as she spoke of it years later.

'Chicago's north side was filled with more Polish immigrants then where my uncle lived. Perhaps he had more friends on the south side, and so the decision to remain here.'

Regionalism played an important role for the immigrant. Life in his community no doubt gave Janek the security he needed in this booming city. So perhaps he also became oblivious to the hovel he lived in. For Babsha, the shock of this community could have gone either way: driven her into deep depression and apathy or strengthened her self-discipline, self-motivation and determination to a higher level. Her obvious fortitude chose the latter.

The rapid expansion of industry in Chicago did not allow for much planning of the neighborhoods that grew along side them.

The hasty plans imposed a trying test of physical and mental stress on the people who lived here. For Babsha and her two daughters, the first two years in Chicago would probably prove the most crucial in determining how they would cope with the remainder of this new life.

'When we finally arrived into this area , the street we would live on, the flat we would rent, the very first thing we noticed was the strange unpleasant odor that filled the air. ' Mama told me. ' "It is the stockyard smell", Uncle Janek told us as soon as he witnessed our wrinkled noses and the way I pinched mine between two fingers.'

Besides this smell, congestion also prevailed in this area. Those who were walking about did so without fancy parasols to escape the sun. No one wore the fine clothing they had witnessed in the business district. No one here rushed around in their day of money making business transactions.

Mama said she could see the disappointed look on Babsha's face as Uncle Janek guided his horse and buggy along the dirt street. When he finally stopped in front of the small wooden unpainted home, Mama said she heard Babsha's heavy intake of breath. 'I am sure she was preparing herself for further letdowns of her high expectations.

'Uncle Janek must have felt her glare long before she spoke. He told us quickly that soon he would be looking for brighter quarters. A place with paved streets and sidewalks. Perhaps something with indoor plumbing as well.'

This area, near 43rd. and Ashland, would eventually be sold to the packers for their expanding plants, as Mama confirmed. 'We did move. In less then a year, but only because we had to. Our relocation, near the corner of 46th. and Ashland, did prove a bit better. In the first home we were all jammed into this little cottage of a small living room, tiny kitchen and one bedroom. The three of us slept in one bed. Uncle Janek slept on three pillows on the living room floor. But he never complained. I think he knew how terribly disappointed his sister was…so he dare not say anything.

'In our new flat, which was a two- story home, our landlord lived in the second floor flat and we in the downstairs flat. He was also Polish and had managed to save enough money from his and his wife's paycheck to purchase this place. Here we had two bedrooms and a much larger kitchen. Although we were still without indoor plumbing, the space gave us more room to breathe.'

A 1939 study of housing in the New City Community Area, which included the Back of the Yards, showed that 15 percent of the housing then standing had been built before 1885; 54 percent before 1915. It was S. E. Gross, a land developer and builder, who organized the subdivisions in the Back of the Yards. Homes that were not only cheaply constructed but cheaply priced as well.

The families that purchased his homes were of moderate means. The wooden one story cottages, with attic and basement sat on twenty-five foot lots. The floor plan was one or two bedrooms, front hall, parlor, a kitchen with pantry…which usually was the largest room of all. The basement, with an outside entrance, could be divided into two rooms and rented. The homes ranged from $1,050 to $1,500. A down payment of $100 and monthly installments of $9 to $11 were affordable for the Back of the Yards worker. With a basement flat bringing rent money, even more so.

Later, when other builders introduced two story frame buildings, more developers followed the trend by replacing small cottages with multifamily dwellings. It was such a unit that the Gajeck family and Uncle Janek moved to from their first flat.

With the rent fairly reasonable in the first flat, Uncle Janek helping with his weekly wages and Babsha bringing in a few dollars by housecleaning in better neighborhoods, finances were just sufficient enough to pay the rent, and perhaps one good meal a day. Yet, from what Mama told me, Babsha never showed any remorse in how her life had changed.

'She was never an overly religious person.' Mama said, 'yet she always made sure Isabelle and I knelt by our bed each evening to say a prayer of thanks to God for bringing us safely to this country of freedom and for the chance we now had to get a good education. She told us many times the decision to migrate to America had been the best one she ever made.'

Sadly, the very thing Babsha hoped to give her daughters in this new world was the one thing they never realized---a completed education.

I am sure Babsha never intended for either of her daughters to quit school at age thirteen and twelve and find a job to help support this struggling family of three. But it was a matter of survival for her when Aunt Isabelle was the first to do exactly that. Two years later Mama followed in the same direction.

Mama always said quitting school was more a blessing then a disappointment. If Babsha did not remain faithful to her Catholicism by attending mass every Sunday, she did show religious concern by sending both her children to parochial school. Where unfortunately, according to Mama, some of the nuns treated immigrant children with contempt. Because Mama could neither speak, read or write in any language but Polish, the few first generation American born children who attended school with her poked endless fun at how the poor immigrant children dressed, acted and at their inability to converse in the country's language. During those early years in school, the nuns in those lower grades only added to her shame by calling her stupid and lazy, for lacking the ability to grasp their teachings with greater speed.

Despite such circumstances, Mama must have been a fairly quick study. Her command of the English language was far superior to Aunt Isabelle's…who spoke a thick broken English at best. In fact, most of our conversations with her had to be in Polish. It was only after her divorce, when she later married a man who was a second generation American, did English finally become the primary language in her home. From what Mama told me, Aunt Isabelle's first husband spoke English fluently. He made sure his children spoke nothing but English. He conversed with Aunt Isabelle in Polish, but abused her both verbally and physically because of her un-American ways. Mama often said one of the happiest days in Babsha's life was the day Aunt Isabelle divorced her first husband.

For other immigrants, the desire to help their parents was one reason boys left school early. For girls, who were destined to become wives and mothers, school seemed a waste of time.

This family of three somehow lived through Chicago's unforgiving winters and relentless hot humid months. By the end of 1918 their combined wages totaled thirty to forty dollars a week—depending on how many homes Babsha cleaned. As 1918 came to a close, the Polish people of Chicago also had much to celebrate. The war had ended and newly resurrected Poland emerged on the map of Europe. Although Uncle Janek was still unmarried, his wages were higher, his job secure. Added to this, this group of four felt lucky and grateful to have escaped the flu epidemic of 1918. Mama only knew of one neighbor who died of this Spanish Influenza outbreak; and only two of Uncle Janek's friends past on from the devastating disease. Babsha always said it was only through sheer luck they had been spared. No doubt that epidemic changed many lives. The next three years would also bring social problems and discord to the Back of the Yards.

In 1915 the increase of Chicago's black population rose to over 50,000 people. This growth was brought on by the so-called wartime great migration.

From the beginning most blacks lived south of the downtown business district. Later, an increasing tendency to have them live in prescribed areas, created the Black Belt on Chicago's south side and a smaller west side ghetto. The word 'ghetto' held a different definition to European immigrants. To them it meant a cluster of ethnic people living in one community. The ghetto that held this newly migrated black populace would become synonymous with squalid living, neglect of property and severe poverty. This connotation, as Tata explained to me, was the result of absentee landlords.

In 1910 Blacks did not occupy more then twelve blocks. Yet in many mixed areas different races lived together in neighborly harmony. This black belt stretched from 12th. Street along State Street as far as 39th. By 1914 the wartime migration of newcomers expanded this area.

Surrounding this belt, hostile whites of working middle class Irish and Jews resented the newcomers. It became a bomb ready to explode. Mama and Tata never discussed the situation of that time to any great lengths. But I am sure Tata and his friends held many discussions during those private hours of smoking and drinking. Mama , on the other hand, although she heard of the deadly crimes of racial and ethnic violence that followed the flu epidemic, was too busy blooming into young womanhood to pay much heed to such things.

'I was sixteen at the time.' Mama explained this time of her life with a twinkle in her eyes. 'With my hair newly bobbed and wearing my first new dress in six years…a lovely beaded mauve, I was too busy attending dances and movies to pay too much attention to racial tensions in Chicago. I loved the music and dancing of the times. Going to the movies and watching Rudolph Valentino, Lillian Gish and Clara Bow on that strange picture screen was a wonderful outlet after working ten hours a day. No, I was never a flapper. The most my Mama allowed me to do was cut my hair. Your Babsha still had the last word on how I dressed and looked before stepping out the door.'

But she always added she could never be totally immune to what was going on outside her neighborhood. Uncle Janek and Babsha talked enough about the riots to keep her abreast of the times. 'Bad enough that homes were getting bombed by rowdy gangs, but when a young black man's death came because he dare cross an invisible boundary existing on the beach of Lake Michigan, Uncle Yanek predicted that the hatred this one white man carried and the riots it created would change Chicago forever. ' Mama's eyes lost their brightness when she spoke of this. 'Sadly, many years later, I realized he was right. But during that time of my youthful years, I only thought of having a good time, working hard at my job and bringing home that little money to help my Mama.'

Mama's new job in a millinery shop paid a better wage then the candy factory where she worked with Isabelle after leaving school. They still lived in the two story flat. Now the street and sidewalks were paved, and their landlord installed indoor bathroom facilities. They still had to trek to the downstairs hallway to use this new convenience, but how much better then trudging outdoors to the dank outhouse or using a pan at night. They were much better off then most families—where three or four families crammed into a two family home shared one bathroom.

Full and complete bathing still remained a ritual that took place at the kitchen sink. When Uncle Janek finally purchased a copper tub and sat it in the kitchen, bathing finally became a once a week replacement for their 'bird-baths'. That they managed to keep reasonably sweet smelling and clean still astounds me. As does the thought of their living conditions during those first years in Chicago. Unpaved streets, clapboard sidewalks, mud clinging to the hem of their skirts…sweat to their clothing on hot, humid days. The thought boggles my mind, since Mama was always so profusely clean. She always insisted on an evening bath and an every day change of clothing. During those hot humid days, as connected to Chicago as wind and severe winters, an afternoon bath and another change of clothing became a common practice in our home.

Our home sparkled clean and always looked orderly. Unwashed dishes left laying in the sink for hours was unexceptable; clothing strewn on the floor was met with quiet scolding. Yet Mama's expectations of cleanliness and order were never so strict that we did not or could not enjoy our living space. She had that special knack in knowing how to allow freedom in an uncluttered environment.

Any wonder that when Leon Kalinowski met her in 1924 he fell in love with her; if not instantly, most certainly soon after.

This five foot four woman had dark brown eyes that twinkled when her cupid lips smiled and a pert nose that added charm to fair unblemished skin as smooth as alabaster. Her hair, the color of rich deep brown coffee, was always marcelled to perfection. All of this certainly enticed the thirty-three year old bachelor. No doubt Tata realized later that all of Mama's other skills and perfections were an added bonus.

There would be one very special quality that probably adhered Tata to Mama and made their marriage last sixty-one years. They were truly inseparable…even in death. When Tata died at age ninety-seven, Mama followed him a year later. As sure as there are angels in heaven, I feel certain they still walk together hand in hand.

To love ones family unconditionally, regardless of faults and differences is one thing. I certainly feel blessed to have had such a family. But Mama's love always went one step further—she rarely said a mean word about anyone, no matter their fault. She was perhaps the most unjudgemental person I have ever known. She was sure everyone had at least one good quality to help us overlook their faults. This, I truly believe, was the one true thing that drew Tata into her web of love.

One might say Mama was philosophical about life and what it had to offer and she loved her family deeply and sincerely. She never complained about her difficult childhood or the fact that she was a working wife and mother for so many years. Spiteful gossip was never a shortcoming of her personality, and gossip was the one thing Tata disliked vehemently. How quickly he must have recognized this shining jewel---how quickly he captured this new found treasure.

THREE MEN FROM POLAND, THE CITY OF GNIEZNO

In 1910, when three young men boarded a steamer bound for America, they had this much in common: all were escaping conscription into the Russian Army and all were handsome and unmarried. Resembling each other remarkably well—all blue eyed, all, except for a boarder of hair at the base of their head, were bald and all carried the same family name…Kalinowski.

Wladyslaw (Walter) was the oldest. His eyes were a deep shade of blue; Stanislaw (Stanley), the youngest, had eyes more blue-green then true blue. The middle brother, Lehon (Leon), was not only the best looking of all three, he also had the most vibrant spirit and the truest blue eyes of all. Pale blue as a robin's egg, Leon's eyes shone as brilliantly as his charismatic personality.

Walter was a bit serious and more then a bit pretentious. Once an aspiring priest, he left the seminary and went on to study medicine. On this day in 1910 he was a licensed practicing physician. His aim in life: to earn enough money and enjoy the comforts of life.

Stanley, an accomplished violinist, had no desire to waste his talent in a Russian army. Like his brothers, he spoke Russian and Czechoslovakian, was fairly well educated, and hoped to make a mark for himself in this new country.

Leon , the least pretentious and most charming of the three, divided life and living into three categories: work, play and rest. He wanted nothing more from life then peace, a bit of good prosperity and the hopeful wish to one day own and operate his own bakery. While working as a bakers apprentice in Gniezno, his future plans certainly did not include the Russian army. Now he planned to make those dreams come true in America. For the moment his plans did not include a wife or family. But one day they would. One day he would become my father. My Tata.

Tata loved life. He relished good food, enjoyed the company of women, was an excellent conversationalist and when he sat down to relax, he meant 'relax' in every sense of the word.

19

I do not know what his parent's did for a living. I do know when the three men left Poland, they left behind a widowed mother and a younger sister. Grandma Kalinowski, according to Tata and the one picture he had of his mother, was a robust, lively woman who loved life and her family to the fullest. She passed away at age ninety-eight. In that same year Tata took full retirement from working outside the home.

His sister Katarzyna remained at home to stay with her mother. Later, when she did get married, she continued living in Poland.

Tata was a prolific story teller. I realized this as soon as he began his account of their crossing to America.

'We had no fear of being rejected at the port of entry.' Tata recounted his story in Polish. A language he would always be more comfortable with, even after many years in America. 'We were more afraid of the Russian police we had to pass at a control station in Germany after our train ride from Gniezno. But the Policeman only eyed us suspiciously and did nothing but return our tickets and allow us through to another room. There we were served rye bread with marmalade, fruit and hot tea.

'After that we boarded a train that took us to the port where a steamer stood docked and waiting for immigrants booking passage to America. My Mamusha cried on that last day at home. But she knew we had to find a new life. She prepared a satchel for each of us filled with buns, raw carrots, boiled potatoes, boiled eggs and jars of tea with plenty of sugar. The very sweetened tea was meant to keep us from getting seasick.

'We boarded the steamer, each of us lugging behind a large trunk filled with our personal valuables. Clothing, linens and fine jewelry. Mamusha received some lovely jewelry during her years of marriage to Tatush. Coral necklaces, cameo rings and broaches. She devided this treasure among all her children on the day we announced our intentions of moving to America. "Perhaps one day." She told us, "you will get married." So I knew she meant these pieces for a future wife.'

For a number of years the jewelry Tata spoke of was kept in his large trunk. All tucked away for safe keeping until he met the wife his mother hoped for him.

'We traveled as third class passengers.' Tata continued. 'And although the deck was crowded with immigrants from all parts of Europe, I felt we were still luckier then the poor souls in steerage.

'When we finally arrived on Ellis Island, our stay only lasted about two hours. The interpreter may have thought we were upper-class citizens. Our exam went quickly. Except for the time it took to change our names, we found no opposition to entering our new country.

'We chose Chicago because we heard from friends that this was a city of 'Polonia'...that is, filled with Poles. Walter especially was anxious to get his shingle out and begin practice on the north side of the city. And Stanley felt sure his skill as a violinist would soon be recognized. As to myself, I hoped to continue as an apprentice in a bakery on the south side.'

My uncle, Dr. Kalinowski, realized his dream rather quickly and easily. When he put his shingle out, this north side of wealthy residents flocked to one of their own kind. Walter Kalinowski found his niche almost immediately.

Stanley was not quite as fortunate. With little room for an aspiring young immigrant musician in a city that had close alliance between artists and entrepreneurs, Stanley found himself excluded from this closely knit marriage simply because he was an immigrant. Because of this he decided early on to move to another city in hopes for better luck. But one disappointment after another finally took its toll on the young man's health. Stanley died at a young age, long before I was born and a few years before Mama and Tata were married.

Tata's fate may have been as disappointing if he had not been viciously determined to make his mark on the south side of Chicago, or if he did not like this city as well as he did. 'Many found Chicago dirty and abrasive, but I saw its beauty.' Tata once told me on on a Sunday morning as we strolled along the lake front.' I fell in love with this city quite easily. The first time I came to fish in this beautiful blue lake was an early Sunday morning. The city was still asleep. I found such peace listening to the singing of early morning birds, the water lapping against the rocks; it reminded me how lucky I was to have found such a place. I wanted to grow with this place…if only in that little part of it on the south side.'

Tata found no openings for a bakers apprentice during those first few years. Undaunted, he chose to work in a tailor shop that, much to his liking, was located on Chicago's south side.

'This end of the city seemed perfection to me.' Tata said as he continued talking about his youth. 'I felt a sense of comradship among the people here. Yes, it was overcrowded, but it was a friendly crowd and everyone had the same goal: work hard and you will reach your goals. I lived in a flat with two other single men and one married couple. His wife did the cooking and cleaning for us. There was a strong bond among all of us. In this part of the city there was a little bit of Poland. Exactly what we needed in a city still so strange to us.'

The tailor Tata worked for was a Polish-Jew. A kindly old man, Tata said, that showed him the correct way to press a pair of trousers, sew on buttons and even do a little mending. The pay was not spectacular, but enough so Tata could put aside some weekly savings.

There were no banking establishments in this area of the city. But an enterprising man in Tata's neighborhood offered savings and loans to all immigrants. Savings earned interest from what the man collected on loan interest. All transactions were kept in empty cigar boxes with the savers name on each box.

Tata stayed with the tailor for three years, during which time he kept a diligent search for a bakers assistant position. His steadfast efforts finally paid off when he found a position as a bakers helper on the north side of the city. It meant he would have to rise at three A.M. every morning. Getting enough sleep meant going to bed at nine P.M. With such a schedule one would think this young man found little time for play. Not so with Leon.

When Tata joined an up and coming Polish choir on the south side, he did so for two reasons: because he loved to sing and because he enjoyed the companionship of men for drinking and smoking and telling stories…and for the company of women as well. In his twenties by now, Tata knew his way around the city. Although an American citizen now, he still spoke very little

English. So because of this communication problem, Leon preferred the company of those men and women in the Polish choir, they in turn found him charming and interesting. Mama attested to his charm many times over. 'He was always a big flirt. He knew how to make a woman feel special. Not only did he love to sing, but dance as well. He had many lady friends. God only knows what other things they loved about him.'were Mama's exact words.

It was in his late twenties—or early thirties, that Tata finally accumulated enough savings to turn his dream into reality.

4936 SOUTH LOOMIS STREET

'What exactly did you think of this neighborhood when you first saw it?' was the question I asked of Tata one day as we sat at the kitchen table. 'The neighborhood was perfect. The bakery shop exactly what I was looking for.' Tata answered. I rather knew what his answer meant. It always seemed so to me as well. The description that follows is one I remember from my early years on this street…perhaps it comes close to what this young man from Poland also saw and fell in love with.

The building Leon looked at sat near a paved sidewalk. Two tiny plots of ground in front of this walk and a cobble-stone street that embraced the entire block of mostly Polish and Czech immigrants. On the peripheral were a scattering of German and Jewish families as well. The Irish would follow later; as well as a small section near Ashland Avenue that would house a Mexican populace.

Most of the homes were two story wood structures with outside steps that led to a second floor flat. A door leading to the downstairs flat was usually located beneath this stairway; then another stairway just inside this door led to the basement and possibly yet another flat. So if the landlord decided to also use the basement as another partial flat that meant he would have a total of three monthly incomes from rentals alone. Of course, most of the time the basement was reserved for doing weekly wash. The laundry was hung on ropes that were strung across the basement from wall to wall.

All of the homes on our block had long walkways to the side of the house. We called them gangways. The gangway led to the back yard and also to another entrance, that may have led to all the flats, including the basement, or only to the basement and the first floor flat.

My remembrance of this area known as The Back of the Yards encompassed an area between 63rd Street south, 31st Street north, Halsted east and Damen Avenue west. It may have been a smaller area when Tata purchased his home on Loomis. Today, the west side boundary extends clear to Kedzie Avenue.

All the homes back then were purchased by Polish, Czech, German, or Irish immigrants. When Tata moved into this area, there was also a small scattering of Jewish people living here. This was evident to me from the retail stores established on Ashland Avenue. Not only Goldblatts and Meyers, both fairly large department stores, but also a fish market, a butcher shop and a jewelry store.

Regardless of who owned what or who lived where, these were a people who had a passion for maintaining this ownership with the utmost care. There were no absentee landlords that one hears of today. Tenants who rented a flat were as tenacious as the owners. Washing windows weekly, sweeping sidewalks and gutters daily, and many times even helping with the repainting of the home. Until that day when people turned to installing siding on their frame homes, which eased the burden of painting, spring house-painting was one sure way of getting to know your neighbors. To this day the smell of fresh paint triggers my thoughts to those spring days when I could be certain to see someone outdoors repainting their home; that sweet clean scent of freshly cut grass and the water from a hose whizzing across it brings back wonderful memories of early morning neighbors rinsing off their lawns and sidewalks. Most back yards were barely big enough to boast a plot of grass let alone any flower beds…yet there they were, bold and beautiful and cared for with love and pride. Our home, being in back of the bakery, had no room for a yard. Like most business establishments, a carpet of green dressed that small plot of ground in front. Something Tata cherished as much as any neighbor with a back yard.

This small area between Racine and Ashland, east to west, and 51st. Street to 47th Street south to north, which would be my playground until I started high-school, held an abundance of grocery stores, the large shopping district on Ashland Avenue, a small scattering of bakeries, Catholic churches that accommodated almost every ethnic group and an over-abundance of taverns. The empty bakery Tata looked at on that one day would soon be called Kalinowski's Bakery. It's address: 4936 South Loomis Street.

The second building from the corner, it sat on a lot 25 feet wide by 100 feet deep. Tata's soon to be bakery shop and new home stood flush against the tavern next door. The most interesting story about Tata's new home was how it came to be on this street.

The front of the house, which was a bakery shop, was the original building built on this site. A fairly large structure, it consisted of the bakery, a baking area, and a small kitchen between the two. The kitchen held a small wood table with three chairs. Before he got married, Tata slept on a cot in this kitchen, cooked on a small stove in this room and ate all of his meals off the little table. He rarely, if ever, used the back of this building for living quarters. The origin of that part of our home was what fascinated me.

When a stockyard company decided to expand, they always bought out a residential block of homes. The homes were either torn down or moved to another area. The back of Tata's home came from such a block. It must have been quite a sight to see a truck pulling a home down the street. But settling it in place was no doubt not only a remarkable feat but an exciting exhibition for those who watched the placing of relocated homes. Especially Tata's home. Whoever added this back part to the front wanted it raised so that the roof was 'architectually' even with the front part.

First a concrete slab had to be poured, with heavy timber beams and concrete pillars set into it. Once set, the new six room house was raised and set on those pillars. A back porch was built and connected this back part to the front. One would enter this back part from the side gangway, open a door to the porch, climb some porch steps to another door. This led to a few more stairs in a small winding hallway that led to another door. This door opened to the first room of the upstairs back flat: a very , very large kitchen, one bedroom to the left , a small bathroom in the corner. Beyond this room, a good size dining room area, one bedroom to the left, a fair size living room, with another bedroom to the side. With an attic above and a garage below, Tata had purchased a fairly large home for himself.

The garage below was entered from the porch, as was the attic above the front part of this home. A large wooden door separated the porch from the garage. I remember how difficult it was for me to run down the little ramp leading to the garage. It was a time when my toddler legs were still unaccustomed to running up and down hills. There was a little room to the side of this ramp that Tata used as a storage area for his baking equipment: cans of lard, large bags of flour, crates of eggs,etc. Ordinarily such items in retail stores would be kept in the basement in the front part of the store. But that basement in Tata's home, which one entered from the small kitchen, housed a large furnace that sent steaming water through all the radiators throughout this home. When coal was delivered, about once a month during the winter, it was dumped in front of our home. Tata shoveled the coal down into the basement through a little door at the front of the building, just below a showcase window. Shoveling that coal down into the basement put a layer of coal dust on everything, hence the reason Tata never used it as a storage area for baking needs. Tata not only had to sweep that black residue in the basement, he had to sweep the sidewalk and hose it down as well. The water hose was kept just inside that little door. It hung on a wall, just to the side, and was quite easy to pull out, then reach in to turn on the water. Needless to say, Tata had himself to clean up as well after the coal delivery and clean-up.

The only time I entered that front basement was to help Tata and Mama in the daily emptying of ashes from the furnace. In the winter when the furnace was in full use, doing its job of warming this large home, I did not mind going down the dimly lit rickety steps. The furnace hissed constantly, and when it came on full blast, the basement seemed rather cozy. In the summer it felt different. Dark and dank and too many spooky images in a child's spirited mind. The attic in the front part of this house also fed my imagination enough so that I stayed clear of it almost completely. I was rather relieved when Mama insisted I stay clear of that attic. 'There are too many loose boards up there. You could easily twist an ankle or break a leg.' Or fall between the boards and disappear, I added to myself. Besides, there was nothing of interest in that attic. Now the back attic, which one entered from a door in the back bedroom, was another story. As was the large garage below the back flat.

So much was stored in that garage: an old dresser with all of sorts of tools, screws and nails. Tata always seemed to find the right equipment in this dresser whenever he had to repair anything around our home. A long table sat in one corner. Mama used this for boning Tata's catch of early Sunday morning fish from Lake Michigan. Long before I was born, it was in this garage that Tata kept a horse and wagon, which he used for delivering bakery goods. Later, when he purchased his first black Ford, and green delivery truck, the horse and wagon were gone. Tata's delivery truck, with the name of his bakery painted boldly in black on the side, sat where the horse and wagon once stood. The reminder of that horse stayed in our garage for a long time. A hook on one of the support beams held an old horse reign and mouth bit. Seeing this I would always conjure up an image of Tata atop his wagon, his horse galloping out of that garage each morning for early delivery of bakery goods. I could almost hear Tata urging the horse to slow down, least they stumble upon someone walking through the alley. An amazing place this garage, almost as much as the attic above the back flat.

An attic with remarkable paraphernalia, especially that which flew: Tata's homing pigeons. His homing pigeons, kept in little wired off houses near a small back window, were part of that attic before Tata married Mama. A hobby that he enjoyed while single. One that Mama tolerated for quite awhile, despite the smell and the mess. Added to that hobby was a beautiful mahogany victrola. Once part of the downstairs living room, Mama condemned it to the attic after she and Tata purchased their first radio console. I loved the amazing sounds that came from that magical piece. Those glorious sounds of Caruso or Rudy Valee floated through the attic, the pigeons cooing almost in unison. And all I had to do was remember to keep turning the handle at its side. While Mama hung her clothes up, on lines strung across the attic, or painstakingly pinned her panel curtains across the special stretchers that stood in the attic, I listened to the music. The perfumed smell of the starch she used for those panels almost obliterated the awful smell of those pigeons…almost.

This was the home Tata cherished. The home he would bring his bride to. A bride that would, for the next sixty-two years, help him in its care and upkeep.

It was an area filled with older immigrants and a few younger ones as well, such as Tata. All wanted nothing more then a good life for their family; nothing less then respect for all of their daily efforts to achieve this goal. The majority of neighbors were outgoing and friendly. That minority that did not care to mingle, or perhaps were a bit apprehensive to do so, nonetheless, always respected any group of newcomers. Of course, there was always that small percentage that was rowdy and at times careless in their behavior toward neighbor.

Tata found this unpleasant percentage in the family that occupied the tavern next door. Koczubowski's tavern stood on the northwest corner of Loomis Street. The family consisted of three boys, young at the time Tata moved into his home, and not old enough as yet to cause problems. Their mother and father ran the establishment of rowdy drinking and weekend celebrations that brought music loud and thumping enough to wake the dead. Tata may have had second thoughts about purchasing his home had he not enjoyed much of the same thing: drinking beer, music and dancing. That thumping sound of Polkas on week-ends hardly made much difference to a bachelor who went out every Saturday. Besides, looking for a neighborhood without a saloon in this part of Chicago, would be like looking for one without immigrants.

Yet Loomis and the surrounding blocks were not as bad as Ashland Avenue with its venue of saloons, which was aptly named, Whiskey Alley. There hard working men (and women) stopped, on that long walk home from work in the stockyards, to have a glass of beer, or two, or perhaps a shot of whiskey…or more, that inexplicable need to talk and vent their wants, their sorrows, perhaps even their joys. In any of the taverns they could find someone who knew exactly what they were talking about. Those understanding companions for the moment, so to speak.

Tata sought the same. He related well to what people were looking for, and accepted the tavern next door. He knew how to talk to the people who frequented his bakery, or the grocer on his delivery route. They were his countrymen, and he got along with them as well as with his neighbors or his friends in the choir.

Neighbors, such as Mr. and Mrs. Kreml, who lived to the south of Tata's home typified more the families that settled in this area. Of Czech decent, and about the same age as Tata, Mr. Kreml worked in the stockyards. His day started as five each morning and ended at seven. Mrs. Kreml stayed at home. It was her job to keep a clean and presentable home for her husband and have a warm meal ready each morning and every evening for her hard working man.

Kreml's home was a two flat frame. Mr. Kreml painted his home every three years. The white trimmed windows were a becoming contrast to the pale gray paint he used on the rest of his house. When Mr. Kreml wasn't painting or repairing something around his home he kept himself busy in the back yard or the small frontage of lawn at the front, as well as that patch between sidewalk and street. But it was the back yard that flaunted colorful flowers and fresh vegetables every spring and summer. Tulips and marigolds bloomed profusely, and Tata's new neighbors would always share fresh vegetables from their garden with him.

The Kremls had one son, Joseph. In later years, after his marriage, Joseph and his wife would occupy the upstairs flat. But now, the Kremls lived upstairs, their neice in the downstairs flat. Libby was a shy young woman with warm velvet blue eyes when she fell in love with her first cousin, Tadeaus.

The young man, visiting from Poland, was tall and handsome and as blond and blue-eyed as Libby. One could immediately guess he came from Mrs. Kreml's side of this family. Her hair, the palest of gold, matched his and Libby's exactly. As did the other features of high cheek bones and blue eyes. I always thought Mr. Kreml, with his almost black hair and coal black eyes a lovely contrast to his wife. No doubt neither ever thought they would have such a dilemma on their hands...that their old maid neice was about to fall head over heels in love with this visitor from back home. Certainly when Tadeaus began to spend more time downstairs with Libby then upstairs with them, their questions began. But it was too late. The two were mad for each other and inseparable two weeks of his arrival.

Mr. Kreml tried to talk them out of a union that would never have the blessing of the church. But the couple was adamant. One month later they were married in the courthouse and evidently lived happily ever after. Except for Mama and Tata knowing the entire story, the affair was kept very quiet. And to ease Mrs. Kreml's mind, who was very distraught over the entire affair, they promised not to have any children. When they moved off to another city, Mama never heard another word about them...or if she did, she never discussed it with Tata. Which was probably better, since Tata hated any sort of gossip. His only remark, when the love affair was revealed to him via Mama, was: 'As long as they are happy, what possible harm are they doing.'

Next to Kremls ever freshly painted home stood a rather morbid looking dark brown home, including the window trim, which made it more stark and dull. This home belonged to Tony and Sally. Both Polish, both immigrants. Tony was a bit older then Tata, a bit shorter, but with more hair on his head that always looked uncombed. His eyes squinted from beneath heavy lenses and dark rimmed glasses. He always seemed in a hurry. In observing his nervous walk as I sat on Kreml's front steps one morning, clamping and tightening roller skates to my shoes, I came to the conclusion that he was forever in escape from his wife, Sally. Crazy Sally, as she was called by my friends and myself.

Sally was younger then Tony. Her mop of red hair looked as wild as his. That alone would have made her more outstandingly noticeable; but it was what she did that gave her that not too nice nickname. When Sally wasn't sitting in her window plucking her brows or talking to the birds, she was yelling at Tony to rake the leaves, sweep the sidewalk or cook her meals. I am quite sure Tony did all of this. I saw him sweep, his sidewalk and gutter as clean as any. I saw him rake. His back yard was not as colorful as Mr. Kreml's, but it had two large trees for marvelous shade, and in the fall, not one leaf covered that lawn. The burning of leaves was an autumn ritual every child in this neighborhood looked forward to. Especially so in front of Tony's home. Once all the leaves from his back yard were piled in the gutter, a match lit to them, the fire under control with his rake and shovel, Tony pulled out about five potatoes from the deep pockets of his sweater and threw them into the hot burning leaves. Sitting to the side, we waited patiently for Tony to find a long sturdy branch, whittle away one end to a fine point, and pluck each potato from its hot nest. Without a word, he passed them out to each of us, only nodding when we thanked him, then going back to his fall cleaning. It seemed the only time Sally never yelled at him, or the only time Tony never rushed to get something done. With all the potatoes he baked for us, his back yard, little front lawn and sidewalk were probably the most leaf-free in autumn. Tony and Sally never had any children. I think now this was the reason Sally left him alone when he baked potatoes for us, or allowed us to help him shovel snow in the winter.

They lived in the upstairs flat of their home. An elderly man lived downstairs when Tata moved into the neighborhood. After that, a couple with a baby. I only remember Stella and her two children, Betty and Bill. Sally was gone by then. If Tony was happier I could never tell. He still rushed around, and still kept everything neat and clean. Stella would be one of the first mother's to display a gold star in her window during World war II.

A small brick building next to Tony's started out as a bakery shop. The owners were immigrants from Czechoslovakia. Their baking specialty was bread and buns and a few sweet rolls. For some reason the bakery was not as successful as Tata's. I hardly ever saw the owners of this bakery, but I did know their daughter. She was about ten years older then me. We often sat and chatted on our front bench. She talked about all her boyfriends. Her name was Marisha, as her parents called her, but preferred to be called Mary. She was quite pretty with her long pale gold hair and green eyes and a most engaging laugh. And quite proud of her prowess capabilities. When she finally did get married, or had to, from what my friends told me, which I never discussed at home, Mary moved away after that. The bakery closed down, but her parents continued to live in the quarters behind the bakery. About the same time, the flat above this bakery was rented out to a young widow with a little boy. Her name was Ann. She called the little boy Jerry. Ann was a plain-pretty woman with curly brown hair and hazel eyes. She did not work and I often wondered how she managed to pay rent and care for her little boy. She spent a lot of time sitting on the front stoop of the doorway that led to inside steps to her flat, and smoking, while her little boy sat on the sidewalk playing with a small wood truck. She always had a lot of company, mostly men. Of course, in my young mind I never guessed what she was doing. Tony seemed to take quite a liking to her and began to spend a lot of time talking to her while she sat outdoors. 'Tony was much older then Ann. Some of the neighbors thought he was having an affair with her, but I believe he was hoping to straighten her life out. He did manage to get her out and working and found someone to care for her son. I felt a bit sad for Tony when Ann moved away. I think he would have been good for her.' So goes the story Mama told me. I only remember that shortly after Ann moved away Tony began seeing another woman. He never remarried. He either loved Sally very much, or she much spoiled the thought of another marriage for him.

Next to the little brick bakery was a long alleyway. It ran from Loomis Street clear to Laflin, the next street around the block. For years this alleyway would be the only one paved and fit for taking a short-cut through. The gray home that stood next to this alley was by far the tallest on this side of Loomis. A three story frame, its landlord was a middle aged man who lived in the downstairs flat. A recluse, he was hardly ever seen by anyone and left the sweeping and caring of his home to renters. A young immigrant couple rented the second floor flat. Both worked in the stockyards. A family with one daughter lived in the third floor flat. The mother went to work only after her husband joined the SeeBees during the war. Their daughter, Lorraine, was in her middle teens when the war broke out and quite a jitterbug dancer. She and her boyfriend won countless trophies for exhibition jitterbug dancing. I was always so envious of her. She was a doll, with her long black curly hair and pale gray eyes, and what I deemed a perfect figure. I always wished I could wear the deliciously bright make-up she wore whenever she went out dancing. How lucky, I also thought, that Lorraine was allowed to stay out late to this all night dancing.

Lorraine married that boy who took her dancing. Two years later they were divorced. It seems he liked to dance with more then one woman.

The next house was a white little frame cottage that I adored, because it seemed so fairy-tale out of place on this block of two and three flat homes. A couple about the same age as Tata lived in this home when he moved on Loomis. Later, it was sold to another couple who repainted it to light brown. At first I thought it would spoil the image, but when they added white shutters and Priscilla curtains across the large front window, I found it even more enchanting.

The couple that bought this home had a little boy. An adorable little boy with a handicap of an enlarged head. Cynthia, and her husband Steve, were hard working first generation Polish-Americans. They adored that child, despite what she said was water on the brain and very difficult to look at and live with, she always added. They were still living in that home when I moved away from Loomis. But shortly after, in a letter from Mama, it said they sold the cottage and moved into a larger home. Cynthia and Steve were expecting another child. Mama asked me to say as special prayer for their new baby. Cynthia never wrote again after that.

Emily and Clement lived in the next frame home with their elderly parents. By elderly, I would say in their fifties…which by standards then, was considered elderly.

Theirs was a two story frame, painted white with dark green trim on the windows. The downstairs flat had an entrance from the front and from a back porch. With an upstairs entrance only from the back porch. Emily and Clement and their Polish immigrant parents lived downstairs. A very elderly couple, bent with age, occupied the upstairs flat. The old man upstairs often sat by an open window reading his paper. There were no screens on windows at this time, and he had to keep shooing the flies away as he tried to read his paper and adjust his glasses. His wife was quite ill and bent with arthritis. After she died, he still sat at the window. But now he had a pillow on the sill, his head upon it, resting and sleeping. No doubt missing the company of his wife in bed.

Clement was two years older then me, Emily about five years older. Their mother and father bought the frame house about the same time Tata moved into his. Clement was an unusual boy with one brown eye and one blue eye. He was shy, perhaps because of this oddity, or so I thought. When Emily began baby sitting for us, I found out exactly why Clement seemed so shy.

Emily was a wonderful sitter…not as good as Babsha, but certainly far exceeding the old man Tata found while delivering bakery goods and who only lasted for one sitting. Mama found him repulsive in his stained overalls and yellow undershirt. He was a short stocky man with yellowing teeth and bad breath. 'What could you have been thinking?' Mama asked Tata the evening they returned early from a dance—which was unusual for them. They enjoyed dancing. But I know Mama hated leaving us alone with that old man. It was the first time I heard her scolding Tata. He only shrugged his shoulders, which was even worse. Through the years Mama would agonize over Tata's keen unwillingnes to participate in any sort of confrontation. He would remain, always, the supreme even tempered man…well, almost always. Except when he was driving and another driver angered him. Then an explosive tirade of swearing, in English and Polish, expelled from him with a swiftness that made me giggle as I sat in the back seat. Mama, sitting with Halina on her lap in the front seat, would always give him a stern look. Thank goodness this display of anger that came clear out of the blue, was rare.

After that fiasco with the old man, Mama found a better sitter—Emily. And it was through her sitting with us that I discovered why Clement was prone to shyness.

Emily, from the way she talked, seemed possessed with the desire to get married. She felt absolutely sure she was doomed to stay unmarried…an old maid. 'When will I ever meet someone to love me and care for me.' Was her constant lament. I mentioned this to Clement one day, as we sat on Kreml's steps. 'That's not the half of it.' He said, and continued to tell me how outrageously Emily flirted with every man they came in contact with and how it embarrassed him, to the point that he wished he could put a bushel over his head every time he went someplace with his sister. His affliction, because of Emily's outgoing personality, became this ingrown shyness. It possessed him as much as Emily's concerns, and both engulfed their lives.

Emily finally did get married. I was about fourteen when I saw her visiting the old homestead with her husband. A tall well-built man, I noted he was as bald as Tata, and quite a bit older then Emily. He showed great affection toward her, his arm around her shoulder, opening the door of their auto for her, kissing her cheek. And it brought one thing to my mind: those smiles she had for Tata—did she pick this somewhat older man because of the feelings she may have had for my father? One never knows.

There was a frame home next to Emily and Clement's house that always mystified me. From what Tata told me, it was a barber shop when he moved to Loomis Street. It still stood as that by the time I grew old enough to take those walks with Babsha. Then suddenly the Barber shop closed, and that shop stayed locked up, forever after. But not empty. A couple lived in the back of this empty store. An unfortunate young pair, because both were ill. One with cancer, the other with a heart condition. She died at a young age. He continued to live a solitary life in that empty store.

The very last building, on the southwest corner of this street, stood yet another saloon. This one belonged to the Wishniewski family. A family of three boys, two girls, mom and dad. The children were first generation Americans, the mother and father immigrants from Poland. This family occupied the entire building. While Koczubowski's tavern was all one floor, with living quarters in back of the tavern, Wishniewski's tavern was a two story building. A large saloon in the front, a room in the rear for dining and holding parties. All living quarters were upstairs.

This was a real family tavern. Patronage and drinking went on every night. Parties of all sorts...weddings, baptisms, First Holy Communion celebration, graduations, even wakes, were held in this tavern. Events held here outnumbered those that were held at Koczubowski's tenfold. All the men in this family were big and tough and so intimidating I never approached the idea of talking to any of them. Yet even though the girls were almost as big and almost as tough, they at least seemed friendlier. Clara was the youngest and the prettiest with light brown hair and big brown eyes. Prone to big bone chubbiness, she nonetheless cared for the way she dressed and looked.

Elizabeth, or Betty, as everyone called her, played and drank like one of the boys. It was only after the war broke out the true spirit of these young people finally surfaced. All the boys enlisted in one branch of the service or another. Betty followed suit by enlisting in the WACS. I will never forget when she came home on that first week-end leave, looking so completely different I hardly recognized her. Slimmed down to a perfect hour-glass figure that showed her small waist and enticing bust, her hair cut and perfectly groomed, she looked marvelously feminine for, what I would say, the first time in her life. While in the army, Betty met her future husband. After the war they moved into one of the flats above the tavern. Clara and her husband in the other. The parents and boys occupied a downstairs flat, converted from the dining area. Between everyone in this building the Wishniewski tradition of saloon keepers lived on. The boys, as far as I can remember, flourished in bachelorhood for just about as long.

Across the street, on the southeast corner, stood Slatky's Grocery Store, and in the upstairs flat, the home of my very best friend, Rosemary. Miss Slatky, Rosemary's aunt, was a tall slim woman with hair pulled back in a tight bun. She always wore a floral print dress and an apron over that. No make up whatsoever, Miss Slatky gave off an aura of cantankerous old maid, since she never married, and her face looked wan and bleak. Nothing was further from the truth. She was the apple of every childs eye in this neighborhood. Miss Slatky never failed to add extra candy to our one or two cent purchases of sweets. A choice always so difficult as we stood in front of that showcase filled with candy.

One became aware of this large showcase as soon as entering her grocery store. It was filled with those marvelous delights of MaryJanes, Root Beer Barrels, Walnettos, Green Leaves, Licorice sticks, and Black Crows. All sorts of all day suckers and my very favorites, little dishes filled with a thick creamy sweet and provided with a teeny spoon for scooping, and those long sheets of paper covered with fabulous confetti-drops of colored candy. Chocolate babies and candy cigarettes became a favorite as I grew older, and tried to act sophisticated with a cigarette dangling from my fingers. Her store was always the highlight of a summer afternoon after hours of roller –skating or playing hop-scotch. During the school year, whenever Mama missed getting to the butchers, she often sent me there after school for slices of cheese or ham. That usually sufficed a snack for Tata between lunch and supper.

The store was, as most retail establishments were, a two story construction. Miss Slatky's living quarters were behind the grocery area. Her grocery supplies kept in the basement. The upstairs flat was occupied by her sister, a brother-in-law and their two children. Although Miss Slatky was a Czech immigrant, her sister was not. Mrs. Gransky was born after her parents and their first daughter arrived in America. That second daughter married Mr. Gransky, an immigrant Czech, and they settled in the flat above the store. They had two daughters, Vivian and Rosemary. Rosemary was born a month before me and would become my very best friend while we were in grammar school and would remain so throughout our first two years in high school.

Slatky's building occupied two lots. The empty lot was filled with more flowers then Mr. Kreml's backyard held, plus two full lilac bushes. Their scent sent a sweetness throughout our block every spring. Miss Slatky was as generous with bouquets of lilacs as she was with penny candy.

Next door to Slatky's was another one story cottage that belonged to Mr. and Mrs. Krason. It sat back away from the street so that the biggest lawn was at the front of the house. They had two sons: John was the oldest and quite different from Eddie, the youngest. John was shorter, stockier and not nearly as handsome as Eddie. Of course, this was strictly the observation and perception of a young and easily swayed young girl. But one could not dispute the gorgeousness of Eddie's thick wavy blond hair, deep blue eyes, and dimpled smile.

This was about a staunch a catholic family as one might imagine. Both boys attended St. John of God Catholic grammar school, while most other children on our block went to Hamline public school. And while Sunday mass was not compulsory in our home, Mr. and Mrs. Krason made sure it was a family affair every Sunday. Of course, none of this deterred Rosemary and me from pursuing Eddie's company. Our endless sessions of playing spin-the-bottle in the hallway of Rosemary's second floor flat was one of the highlights of summer fun. One summer we were bold enough to suggest playing 'doctor' and 'patient' with Eddie. We got as far as listening to our heart beat with a play stethoscope. Rosemarie tried to get Eddie to pull off his shirt, but her urging was unsuccessful. I am sure Eddie realized the next step might be removing his knickers. At any rate, our childish efforts proved fruitless and we never pursued the game any further, not that summer or any other. For a long time I felt sure we were the ones to dissuade Eddie from any future relationships with women.

Eddie entered the army right after high school graduation. The armed forces proved too stressful for this young and gentle man. Within months he was released with a medical discharge, and soon after joined a seminary. He always told me his mother and father hoped he might become a priest, and so he did. Although he looked quite handsome in his black religious garb, I felt for a long time the best outfit for Eddie may have been a black tux, with me in white standing next to him.

The best kept home on our street, at least in my point of view, had to be the one next to Eddie's. A one family frame, painted white with bright green trim, it belonged to the only Irish family on our block. A quiet family with two husky boys that would go on to become Chicago firefighters. I do not remember them as well as they remembered Mama and Tata. After my

40

parents moved to Tucson to live with me, it would be here that my Tata died. Unknown to us, the one firefighter that lived in that home, also moved to Tucson after his retirement. When he read the obituary and saw Leon Kalinowski's name listed, he attended the mass we held on the day of Tata's funeral. A small world indeed.

When he approached Mama after mass, hugged her and told her who he was, Mama's. tears came quickly. I know her memories were overflowing the day of Tata's funeral. When that retired firefighter reached out and held her I am sure she remembered that home she lived in as a young bride and the neighbors who gave her so much joy. I have forgotten completely what his name is. I wish now my memory bank had been more alert on that day. Perhaps our paths will cross again. But I do remember how that family sat at the top of those green and white steps, waving to all the children as they roller skated by on summer days.

Another large three story home sat next to the firefighters house. Not quite as tall as Lorraine's home, it sat back away from the front sidewalk and boasted a large front lawn. This lawn about the only one not too well cared for as others on our street. The home was painted light gray with dark gray steps and window trim. I never remember it being occupied by more then just one man. A strange man at that, and one I noticed on the first Halloween Mama allowed me to go out trick or treating. Rosemary, Eddie, Clement and I were just approaching this gloomy looking home with shades always drawn, when we saw the owner drive up in his newly purchased auto and park it along the curb in front of his home. We sat on the firefighters green steps, Rosemary dressed as a princess, Eddie and Clement as bums, and me in my usual dress and hat Mama discarded for Halloween dress-up. We sat and watched, mystified, as the man stepped out of his black car, locked the door and then stood there waving his arms and muttering some sort of prayer. He walked around the car several times, chanting some ritualistic tune, stopped a few times to recheck the car door and then proceeded to go inside his home. The man himself looked rather odd, with stooped shoulders, a mop of wild white hair, and clothing that always looked rumpled. No one knew where he worked or what his name was, but Tata said the man lived in that house long before Tata moved on Loomis.

None of us dare venture unto that front lawn or climb those dark gray stairs that led to the front door. I myself could hardly wait until I got home to relate this strange scene to Mama and Tata. Mama thought the man must be quite lonely and said perhaps we may have been wiser to knock on his door and introduce ourselves. Tata was more philosophical when he expressed his thoughts to me in Polish.: 'perhaps it is the man's first auto. No doubt he was entranced by its performance and was talking to it.'

'And you do not think this strange?' I asked him.

'We all have strange behaviors. He harms no one in what he does, so we must accept the difference.' Tata explained. Which to me was a good explanation that helped confirm my belief that the man was perhaps missing something in his head that made him so different and curious. Of course, to a child, everything is black and white: there were those who did the right thing, and those who did the wrong thing. Those that were sane, those that were insane. Life was simple at that age. Reality would come later in life. That home and that man remained a mystery to me until the day Mama noticed his car stood outdoors for a couple of days, without going anywhere. She decided to take some bread and sweet rolls over to him, concerned that perhaps he was ill and unable to go out. The air was quite chilly, the wind whistling winters close arrival when Mama stood on that front porch and knocked on his door. I sat on Kreml's steps, watching over her, for fear he might pull her into the house and we would never see her again. When the front door finally opened I sat up straight and held my breath.

The man looked so little, standing there in a ragged robe that matched the gray house. He nodded when Mama handed him the bag of bakery goods. They stood and talked for a little awhile. When he sat the bag down and reached out to hold Mama's hand, I stood, ready to run across the street to help Mama. But nothing happened. Mama just kept nodding her head, while the man kept hold of her hand, his head bobbing up and down, his white hair blowing in the wind. Finally, he picked up the bag, and closed the door behind him. Mama stood there for awhile before she finally came down the steps and returned to where I sat watching.

I could see her face was streaked with tears. 'Is everything all right Mama?' I had to ask. I had to know. Mama came and stood in front of me. 'Yes little one, everything is fine. His wife and child died on the voyage across the ocean. He has been alone ever since. Tell your friends to treat him kindly. He is a very lonely soul.' The mystery may have been solved for Mama, for me there was more to puzzle over then ever before. Our mystery man moved away two years later. The house stood empty for years after, until a family of eight bought it. It look lively after they repainted it pale yellow.

Elaine and her widowed mother lived next door to the mystery man house. Elaine's father died just shortly after they moved into this two family home with a basement. He was a German immigrant and married Elaine's mother shortly after arriving in America. Elaine's mother worked outside the home, in the stockyards. A woman of medium height and fine boned, I thought she had a rather pretty face despite the fact she always looked drawn and tired. Elaine obviously resembled more her German heritage: large boned, but slim, she kept her dark blond hair long with bangs that almost covered her eyes. Eyes that stayed narrow and seemed to constantly flit about, ever cautious of approaching doom, as Mama once observed. Although I could never imagine Elaine being afraid of anyone or anything. Elaine had a personality that turned quickly from sweetness to toughness in a blink of an eye. Besides this, she was considered a 'fast-girl', which, during this period in time, meant she had lots of boy friends visiting her when she was home alone. Four years older then me, I was totally frightened of Elaine after I saw her beat up a girl who called her a name very unfamiliar to me.

'What is a whore, Mama?' I asked after that incident.

'Not a very nice name to call anyone. Especially Elaine.' Mama said, after I told her what had happened. 'She has had a very hard life. Her father gone, her mother working all day. We have no right to judge her so quickly just because she seeks

43

company and that company happens to be a few boys she befriended in school. Perhaps the girl who called her such a name is just jealous of Elaine's popularity.' Mama's explanation made sense, but still, I was afraid to approach Elaine. I might say something to offend her and get beaten up as well. Eventually I did talk to her, but always with caution.

It was after the war started that I finally got to know Elaine so much better. She married young man that lived just two blocks away. He was in the army and had to leave Elaine shortly after their marriage. She had a baby boy while he was gone and continued to live with her mother. When Elaine's husband returned from the war, fully discharged now, he had one arm missing. Elaine never faltered from the love she had for this tall, almost too thin man she called her 'darling husband'. They settled in the downstairs flat after a Greek family moved out. Their life continued quite happily.

'You see how she was misjudged?' Mama reminded me one day. 'To live up to the name she was called, this settled life would have never happened.'

The two-story home next to Elaine's had a flat upstairs one entered from stairs just inside a front downstairs door. Owned by two sisters, one a widow, the other an old maid, it seemed destined for young couples to live in the downstairs flat. Young couples, childless or with children, always occupied that flat. Eventually, my own son and his family would do so also. I have come to the conclusion that the women who owned this home found great enjoyment in seeing young people begin there life in this home. Perhaps they considered it good luck. By the time my son and his wife moved in, only the widow was left to tend to this property.

Next was a two story frame that belonged to a couple in constant disagreement. I was awed at the sight of 'her' throwing dishes at 'him' as he scurried down the front steps. Even more awed at how many times the cops had to come out to put a stop to their disputes. Surprisingly, whenever they went for an evening walk, they did so hand in hand and looked perfectly normal. They moved out just before I started third grade. The couple that moved in was much more peaceful.

The little elderly Polish couple that lived in a small white one story/single flat cottage next to the house of noise, showed the devotion a long happy marriage brings. They swept their front sidewalk together each morning...she doing one side, he the other. They walked hand in hand to Sherman Park, for their weekly baths...each with a towel in hand, walking slowly, she holding on tightly to his bent arm. They were so adorably in love, and so frail looking. They always said good-morning to Mama and Tata and came to our bakery at least once a week for bread and sweet rolls. They paid little regard to other neighbors, Tata said perhaps out of fear. Especially after the police came around for the arguing couple. Tata thought perhaps this elderly couple came from Russia, since their last name ended with a 'y'. 'Perhaps they once felt the sting of the Russian Cozaks, a group much feared in Russia. And if this is true, I can say they must feel very lucky to be living in America now.' At any rate, they were a very quiet couple; their home well cared for.

The home next to the elderly couple always confused me...not the home...the people who lived in it.

It was a well kept home. With two flats and that extra flat in the basement, where the grandmother lived. Her son, Mr. Jankowich, his wife and their daughter occupied the first floor flat. The second flat was used as a sewing room and reading room for Mrs. Jankowich and her daughter Anna. Anna was about two years older then me and attended St. John of God School. I never got to know her, simply for the fact that she, as did her mother and father, considered themselves too good for our neighborhood.

Mr. and Mrs. Jankowich were what we would call today, workaholics. Both were employed outside the home, and both worked around their home nonstop...after work as well as weekends. Their home was not any more well kept then the firefighters home, which was meticulously perfect, but Mr. Jankowich, from what Mama once told me, demanded perfection. When Anna fell in love with a boy from our neighborhood, Mr. Jankowich was not too pleased. But John, Anna's choice, and a friend of mine as well from high school days, finally convinced the father that he would give this girl the same quality of life her parents had so ordained. Anna and John bought a home on the north side, no doubt in a much classier neighborhood then ours. This was a family quite obviously living in the wrong neighborhood. Perhaps they knew this, and rather then accept life as it was and enjoy what they had, their dissatisfaction fed their need to work to such a ridiculous extent.

The last building, just across from Koczubowski's tavern, was another grocery store with two flats above. One outside door, downstairs, gave access to both flats.

This was a very old-fashioned grocery at its finest: barrels filled with pickles, rice, beans, cracker, etc. A very small store, it had a showcase with only a fraction of the kind of candy at Slatky's. But later, it would acquire a small freezer that held flavors of vanilla, chocolate and strawberry ice cream. Surprisingly, it also became the first store to sell wrapped white bread.

The Polish immigrant couple who owned this store were called Gorale, the Polish word for peasant. Both had olive skin, black hair and eyes that were such a deep brown they looked almost black. Mama told me this Polish sect was comparable to the Appalachian Hill people of America. And like the Appalachians s were also stereotyped at being downright lazy, not very clean and uneducated. With Mr. and Mrs. Gczobek, nothing could be further from the truth. As Mama always said, what one is, is what one is taught to be.

Mr. and Mrs. Gczobek were probably the second oldest couple on our block. They kept their store and their surroundings immaculate. Floors were scrubbed daily, windows sparkled brightly. They had a large turnover with their upstairs tenants, only because it took awhile for this couple to find families clean enough to satisfy their demands. The food they sold was not as modern as Miss Slatky's, but whatever they kept or sold in their grocery store was clean and tasty.

So then, this was the neighborhood Tata moved into. Where on warm summer nights families sat outdoors in conversation with neighbors or in silence with their own thoughts. Where the sound of children laughing and playing hide-and seek mingled with the sound of crickets and Polka music from two taverns.

Where glowing stars above and one or two dimly lit lampposts competed with twinkling fireflies. Where a sleepy-head child heard the distant sound of church bells each morning at six, where a worker stopped to eat when that same bell tolled at noon, and a catholic stopped to make the sign of a cross as the bell rang six p.m. vespers. During cold winter nights, when except for the howling of Chicago wind, or the distant sound of a train, Tata's home became his quiet and peaceful domain. Frosty windows, the fresh fallen virgin white snow sparkling bright in winter…a place to sit outdoors and visit on warm summer evenings.

But those quiet nights, summer or winter, could get very lonely for a man who enjoyed company. For a man who wanted a wife to love and to care for him. For a man who wanted to be a husband and share his good luck; who hoped for a family to carry on his beliefs.

So what was it that finally attracted Mama to this Polish immigrant who spoke the most minimal amount of English…who certainly was not outstandingly good-looking, with his bald head, but had the most electrifying blue eyes? Was it the little mustache Leon kept neatly clipped above full enticing lips? Or perhaps his very charismatic personality? He was, after all, a good talker, a sincere listener and a man very sure of what he wanted from life. Perhaps it was any one of, or all of these things that made Tata so endearing to all who met him, as well as to Henrietta Gajeck. But I believe there was that one thing that made him stand out as special in Mama's eyes: his tenderness and calmness. Tata always had the composure of a good captain that remained unfluttered despite the storm around him. As an example, Mama once asked him, this after quite a number of years into their marriage, how he could sit so calmly, reading his Polish paper, while outdoors the snow, coming down relentlessly, covered every sidewalk, including ours. Mama could not bear the thought of people trudging through so much snow. Tata answered her in his most logical and unperturbed manner: 'God put that snow there, and I am sure He will make it melt as well.' Of course, Mama being Mama, only shook her head, put on her warm coat, boots, scarf and mittens, and went out to shovel the snow.

I am sure Tata's lack of stress over what he considered a silly problem and his lack of worrying over things that had not even happened was a constant dilemma for Mama. I know through the years she nagged him...a delightful nagging I call it now, for it went in one ear and out the other. As Tata grew older, we felt sure his hearing was going bad. We found out soon enough it was only 'selective'. And so it was this quiet, unassuming, certainly very unpretentious man named Leon Kalinowski, that Mama truly fell in love with.

LOVE, MARRIAGE AND FAMILY

Most horse traffic disappeared by 1918. By 1922 one could see the impact of the automobile on this growing metropolis of Chicago. Rush hour traffic, electric traffic signals, now a familiar problem of the motorist. But the traffic of Michigan Boulevard and other streets in Chicago's Loop were hardly noticed on the still cobble stoned Loomis Street. The city only paved those streets to accommodate upper-class residents. Not that it bothered Tata or anyone else in this area. The city had at least lined their walks with young maple trees. Quiet streets that were pleasantly peaceful. Especially during those hot summer evenings when everyone sat outdoors for longer spells.

Babsha and her family were feeling the same sense of gratefulness. Ten years now since their arrival to this new country. Henryka was working full time and Uncle Janek prospering well in his employment. And now they lived in a flat with more suitable surroundings. Chicago, despite its wicked and corrupt elegance of favoritism, had given all of them a livable and fairly happy life.

Mama was nineteen years old. I surmised she felt some of the beauty and excitement of this growing city when she told me how much she loved to go dancing...the Charleston, the Lindy Lou. As she spoke of these youthful days I could visualize the lovely young girl with dark hair and charming cupid lips enticing many young men as her legs moved, skirt twirling around her legs while she danced away. Despite her ethnic upbringing, Henrietta loved the music of the day: Baby Face; Ma, He's Making Eyes At Me; Toot, Toot Tootsie Goodbye and scores of others, which I recall her singing as she worked around the house. She idolized movie stars such as Pola Negri and Valentino, and much to Babsha's objections, had her hair cut and marceled. 'But she really put her foot down when I tried to shorten my skirts. ' Mama reminded me of her strict upbringing. 'I settled for a pair of lovely long beads instead, which Uncle Janek bought for me.'

Aunt Isabelle, divorced by now, was living at home again with her two children, Edward and Alfreda. Within six months she would remarry again to George Cregier. A man far gentler then her first husband. Uncle George was a first generation American and quite liberal in his sexual orientation. Before he married Isabelle he wanted to make sure she was capable of bearing children for him. When she did become pregnant with my cousin Herbert, or Herby as we always called him, he then married her. Three years later they had Madalaine. The entire family settled in a lovely brick apartment on the north side of Chicago.

When the Volsted Act was passed by congress, this provided the enforcement for the 18th. Amendment which made it illegal to manufacture, transport or sell any beverage containing one-half percent or more of alcohol. Prohibition went into effect on January 16, 1920. Tata, by every indication in the stories he told, could care less.

He had friends who frequented enough speakeasy's to provide him with the whiskey he needed to make his own sweet liqueur. Not the moonshine or bathtub gin so many took to making; his was a cherry-sweet sophisticated, scrumptious drink that felt like pure velvet on the palate and went down the throat like warm smooth honey. Tata continued making this exquisite brew for many years after prohibition ended. It became a ritualistic before dinner drink whenever Tata and Mama had company...regardless of a surprise visit or planned invitation. Family and friends knew they could drop in for a visit at anytime. No one had to wait to be formally invited.

1922 was a period of prosperity for the country. By 1924 Tata's bakery was flourishing. He was very active in the Polish Choir and the people he met from this group of young Polish men and women continued in his friendship throughout most of his life.

The drinking, dancing and off-color jokes while they sat around and smoked their cigars or cigarettes, was the highlight of Tata's week-end entertainment. Although he never admitted the fact to me, Mama attested that Tata also frequented the red-light district on Garfield Boulevard. This area of the once rich and prominent, the boulevard was lined with large brick homes, the street paved, now belonged to 'high-class' madams, and a new conquest for any young man seeking excitement.

But that sort of newness lasted only a short spell for Leon. With his life focused more on the realities of life, he soon found such exploits boring and dull. Once again his thoughts became filled to settling down with a good wife.

Mama joined the same choir Tata belonged to. It was 1926. Henrietta Gajeck was twenty-three years old and joined this choir only at the insistence of Babsha, who thought it best if her daughter mingled with people of her own rather then the 'roaring twenties' crowd. 'We obeyed our parents in those days. My marceled hair and the clothing I wished to wear, and could not, no doubt told my mother that it was time I mixed with a different crowd. At first I missed those dances at the Midway Garden on Cottage Grove, and the friends I had there. But I knew this Polish Choir would be the best place to meet a man suitable for marriage.'

Finding that 'right man' did not take very long. Henia, as Tata always preferred calling her, met Leon during her first choir practice. Within a month they were engaged. Mama's favorite precious metal jewelry was always white gold. Uncle Janek told her once it was best suited for her pale skin, dark eyes and hair. No doubt he also mentioned this to Tata, for when he presented Mama with an engagement ring, it was a lovely setting in white gold.

On December 27, 1926, Henryka Gajeck became Mrs. Leon Kalinowski. Their ceremony was performed by the Justice of Peace in the courthouse of downtown Chicago. Aunt Isabelle stood at her side as Matron of Honor and Tata's brother, Dr. Kalinowki, as Best Man. Only minutes before, Leon had been a bachelor in his middle thirties. Now he would be bringing not only a wife to his home on Loomis, but a mother-in-law and Mama's Uncle Janek as well.

As adept as Tata was in making his bakery a success, his living quarters were another matter altogether.

Certainly Mama had seen the bakery and the baking area in the time period of their engagement. But Tata never once suggested she go upstairs to the second flat. Not that it would have shocked her; after all, unpainted floors and meager living conditions were nothing new to her. But with the friends Mama made throughout her time, in that crowd of people that lived in better neighborhoods, she now knew what changes could be made in this new home. And the new groom was willing to please his bride.

The unpainted connecting porch was probably her first clue to what she might encounter in that upstairs flat.

Those steps matched every unpainted wood floor in every single room of that six room flat. Although there was a bathroom off the kitchen, with a chain-pull flushing toilet, there was no tub. And even though the kitchen did have a little sink for washing dishes, there were no closets in which to hang any clothing. More, Tata always used the large kitchen for hanging up his weekly wash. The rope strung across this kitchen must have been the second eye-sore Mama encountered.

Walls were unpapered, or had peeling paper, windows were bare of either curtain or shades. 'When I saw the size of this flat, none of this bothered me. All I could see was how this place could be turned into a lovely home for my new husband and our family. I also knew Tata wanted to please me.'

By the time I was born, on February ninth, 1928, Mama's new home came close to being exactly what she wanted.

I came into a world that had also seen quite a few changes: people were now working the forty-hour work week, which was introduced by Henry Ford. Mama's movie idol, Valentino died in 1926 and that same year the first motion picture with sound (music only) was introduced. In 1927 Tata bought the newly introduced Model A Ford and the wealthiest gangster in Chicago was a man called Al Capone. In the year of my birth, Al Jolson starred in The Jazz Singer. It was the first official 'talkie' movie.

Herbert Hoover was elected President of the United States in this same year. And an animated character by the name of Mickey Mouse was introduced by Walt Disney. Downtown Chicago, known as 'The Loop', was lined with giant skyscrapers and busy streets. It was the heart of the city. To Tata and Mama and their newly arrived daughter, Loomis Street was the heart of the city in their eyes.

The name on my birth certificate read: Przeslawa Leonia Kalinowski. Tata insisted on using my middle name in every day life, and from the beginning I was known as Lonia. I was baptized at St. John of God Catholic Church, and afterwards Mama and Tata had a splendid gathering of friends and family in their newly redecorated flat.

Stairs, walls and flooring on the connecting porch were painted off-white. Three small windows on that porch were covered with curtains. The small hallway leading to our large kitchen was equally painted, a small window covered with a dark ecru shade. In this same hallway, a good size green ice-box sat and was now filled daily with a block of ice, delivered to us by the ice-man. This ice-box once occupied the downstairs kitchen, while Tata was single and only used that one room. When Mama entered his life, moving that box was one of the first changes she made. Mama needed that ice-box close to the kitchen that would now be used every day.

Inside the flat, all the floors, including the bathroom, were covered with linoleum rugs; the wood edging around the rugs painted brown. Radiators were repainted with silver paint. Shades and paneled curtains covered all of the windows. And best of all, a bathtub was added to the bathroom.

A small, black, pot-bellied stove was installed in one corner of the kitchen, just before one entered the dining room. The flames flickering behind those crackling little isinglass windows always fascinated me. That little stove made our kitchen the coziest room in that entire flat.

Tata had two closets built against two walls of the kitchen; in between, a large walk in existing pantry. This pantry always stayed unbelievably cool in the summer and very cold in the winter. Whatever Mama did not have to keep in the ice-box, was kept in this pantry. Above a radiator in our kitchen there was a little window. It opened up to Koczubowski's flat roof. During our frosty cold winters that flat roof was a perfect outdoor ice-box for much of our perishable food. All Mama had to do was stand on the radiator, open the small window and set out whatever she needed kept cold. Of course, that only worked during cold winter months. In the spring and summer that block of ice continued to be delivered each morning. Beneath the ice-box sat a pan. It caught the melting ice and had to emptied at least twice a day during warm months; once or every other day during cooler months. The hallway between porch and kitchen door felt as cold as the outdoors during winter months. During the summer…it was as warm or hot as the outdoors, and that ice in the box melted quickly.

Mama's pride and joy was her mahogany dining room set. Tata surprised her with this gift on their very first wedding anniversary. The pieces consisted of a large table that expanded whenever we had company; six chairs—four that sat around the table at all times, and two others that sat next to a long buffet. Mama kept her best china and glassware in that buffet. Every piece of that dining set was polished with oil on every Friday during house cleaning. The shine so high I could see my reflection in that rich dark wood.

The entrance to the living room was divided by two columns, with two low cabinets attached to each. Through the years Mama would receive gifts of glassware and small dishes which she stored in each cabinet. On the very lowest shelf of one cabinet Tata kept his drinking supplies and of course that special liqueur. Mama's best silverware, which she received as a gift from Uncle Janek, was kept in a box and on the highest shelf in the pantry. All of her fine dining utensils were brought out twice a year…for Christmas Eve and Easter Sunday, and for such occasions as a baptism.

Our living room always looked fresh and cozy with its long radiator against three large windows that overlooked the alley below and a fine tall gray home that was actually around the corner on 49th. Place…so our windows faced the side of this home. When I was born the living room floor was still covered with linoleum. Soon after Tata purchased two rugs, one for this room and the dining area as well. Our flat was never overwhelmed with furniture. A wood table and chairs in the kitchen, the dining room set, a sofa and two chairs, two standing lamps, a little later the console radio that came with its own little stool, and a rocking chair.

The three bedrooms of this flat stayed the same during my earliest years of life. Mama and Tata slept in the bedroom off the kitchen, probably because this was the only bedroom that had a door for privacy. Babsha slept in the bedroom off the dining area, a bed I shared with her while Uncle Janek was still living with us. He slept in the bedroom off the living room area. But soon some of this would change.

Janek Macherzynski finally did meet the woman of his dreams. While visiting a friend he worked with, Uncle Janek was introduced to a tall, older then he woman, whose name was Mania Prestolka. She was a widow with two daughters, Elsa and the youngest always known as Baby. Mania owned her own home, a three flat brick on the north side. Uncle Janek was no doubt impressed. Within three months of this first meeting they were married. We always called her Ciocia Mania, which translated means, Aunt Mania. I adored her. Next to my Babsha she was the most down to earth adorable woman I ever knew. Her marriage to Uncle Janek could not have come at a more opportune time. I was three years old and Mama was expecting her second child.

From what Mama told me, Uncle Janek broke the good news of his meeting with Mania while Mama was in the midst of her Monday wash. Mama washed clothes every Monday in her green ringer-type washer. The washer was kept in a corner, next to the pot belly stove. Every Monday, while Tata tended to the bakery store, Mama would roll that wash machine over to the kitchen sink. After attaching a long hose to the kitchen faucet, she put the other end inside the machine, turn on the faucet and wait until the machine filled up. Meantime, Mama would slice off pieces of naphta soap and drop it into the machine. Only after the machine was full of water did Mama plug its cord into an outlet and start the agitator with a press of a button. By the now she had hot water and for a long time marveled at the convenience of this…rather then heating pots of hot water on the stove…or doing all the laundry on a scrub board. Still, this Monday wash took most of the day. For afterwards, she had to carry the wet wash upstairs to the back attic and hang each piece carefully on lines strung across from wall to wall. Then the emptying of the washer...wiping it out thoroughly as well as mopping up any water on the floor in this area...which was a given.

I always enjoyed going up into the attic with Mama on wash day. If for nothing more then to watch the pigeons flying in and out of their cubbyholes. That enjoyment came to a sudden end.

Mama hated the smell of those pigeons. She complained about it to Tata after every Monday wash and every Tuesday when she went up there to bring her wash downstairs for ironing. She finally convinced Tata that the odor permeated the entire downstairs flat as well. He got rid of those pigeons just before my sister Halina was born. A friend from the choir lived in the country now, the pigeons would be better off, Tata told me the day they were carted off. Besides, Babsha would now occupy the back bedroom, all the more the pigeons had to go...that room, according to Mama, smelled the worst. Apparently Uncle Janek never paid much attention to the smell. And now he would be moving to a fine brick home on the north side of Chicago.

I enjoyed all my visits with my new cousins. Baby was much more fun then Elsa, who always seemed a serious young woman...reading, attending all sorts of clubs, and really not as adorable as Baby. Her short curly blond hair and large blue-green eyes were a perfect match to a bubbly personality. Baby was eighteen years old when she found the love of her life. I only remember that he was tall and dark and very handsome. I was more thrilled at standing up to Baby's wedding as a flower girl. At age eight, this would be my first long dress for this special occasion: pale lavender, and the bouquet of flowers I carried matched the dress perfectly. Baby was the first and only bride I ever knew that wore a pale blue wedding gown...and she looked absolutely scrumptious in her unusual wedding attire.

I mentioned this unusual color of wedding dress to Emily, who always spoke of what her white wedding dress would look like. Emily raised her brows and said, 'perhaps your cousin was not a virgin.' Since I had to idea what that meant, I let the remark go in one ear and out the other. Later, when I heard stories about Elaine and her supposed escapades, I began putting two and two together and wondered just how popular Baby had been before she got married.

My week-end visit to Aunt Mania's and Uncle Janek's home are remembered with warm and tender fondness. She was a marvelous cook. A Polish immigrant, she came to this country at a much earlier age then Mama. Her first husband was a second generation American and quite wealthy. Aunt Mania's cooking was far more Americanized then Mama's. I tasted my first lasagna during one of those visits, as well as large helpings of golden fried chicken. After any of the enchanting meals Baby would always take me for a long walk. We always stopped at a store for an ice-cream cone. Mama never had to coax me to visit with my aunt and uncle.

Uncle Janek seemed so perfectly content and happy at last. 'He and Mania did everything together.' Mama told me. 'He seldom saw his friends after that marriage. He told me once he never realized how empty his life had been until he met Mania.'

Sadly, the marriage ended about four years after Baby's wedding. Uncle Janek died rather suddenly. Tata said it was pneumonia. I continued my week-end visits, but that stopped after a short while. Their home seemed so empty and quiet without Uncle Janek. Elsa was always gone and now that Baby was married, I found Ciocia Mania's solitude too depressing. Perhaps I was changing as well. Just as the world around me.

By the time my sister Halina was born, our bathroom floor was tiled in pretty little black and white tile that felt like little stones to me when I held one in my hand before it was laid in place. Tata also had a new and modern flush toilet installed. Now we no longer had to stand and pull the chain of a box above to flush.

There was much excitement in our home the day Halina was born. Just as I, she came into the world in Mama's bed. Only where Babsha helped in my birth, Dr. Kalinowski assisted in Halina's.

We did not visit much with my uncle, the doctor. Mama never said why she did not like visiting there or talking to her sister-in-law. It was only after my uncle died that Mama said it was too bad his wife felt she was so much better then the relatives on her husband's side. 'She always put herself above the people that lived on the south side.' But yet, I do remember clearly one visit to that home. It was after their young daughter, Jenush died, and Tata went there to console his brother.

Dr. Kalinowski had two daughters, Jenush, the oldest, and Hannah, the youngest, whom we always called Hania, also a son named Leczack, or Larry. When Jenush died from complications after a ruptured appendix, my uncle was terribly distraught that he, as a doctor, could not save his own child. Whether Tata helped him any emotionally Mama never said, but I do remember going over to that home that one day and seeing the portrait of Jenush on a wall and my uncle weeping as he sat in a chair beneath it.

My cousin Hania visited with us quite often after that on week-ends.. Her visits came during one of those memorable Midwest Indian Summers that enticed maple leaves into turning gold, kept our days comfortably warm and brought a touch of autumn to evening air.

When Tata drove us to Western and 87th on those Saturday week-ends for an enjoyable evening of Rainbow ice-cream, it seemed so far away from where we lived. The large red building was always crowded with parked cars and lines of people waiting to experience the luscious large spoonfulls of various sherbet flavors and vanilla ice-cream heaped into a big crispy cone.

I enjoyed Hania's visits. She was older and seemed so much more sophisticated then I was. She kept her beautiful reddish-brown natural curly hair long, and the clothes she wore always looked so expensive. We always had so much to talk about...school, movies, and how different her life was from mine. The visits came to an abrupt end. My uncle grew ill and had to give up his practice. He died shortly after that. I never visited that home again, nor did I ever see Hania again. Mama did keep in touch with her after Hania married and moved to another state.

As brothers are different, so too can sister's be very opposite...in looks and personality. As Halina and I were, and are to this day. I was the oldest, and expected to act more adult, and have more sensibility. Being the youngest, and having inherited the pert prettiness of the Gajeck women, my sister was always somewhat spoiled. Not a nasty spoiled, for Tata would never allow that. But spoiled enough to make her adorable and favored as any baby of any family. That favoritism ended the day Halina took a pair of scissors to Mama's finest silk hosiery.

Halina was about three years old at the time. Her demands started early this one morning, and Mama, being very busy on this day, had little time for such foolishness. When my sister began a crying fit and stomping her little feet, Mama took her by the arm and led her to the bathroom. This was the only other room besides Mama's bedroom that had a door. Mama was not about to put Halina in that bedroom, where she would jump up and down on Mama's bed, as she had done many times before. So the bathroom it was.

'When you come to your senses, you can come back out.' Mama instructed as she closed the bathroom door behind her, Halina inside, still wailing. That went on for about ten minutes. Then all grew quiet. 'I thought that stay in the bathroom had finally stopped those tantrums…how wrong I was.' Mama told me once during our talks.

Early that same morning Mama had rinsed out a new pair of silk hose. A small pair of scissors she used to open the package still lay atop the bathroom sink. The new hose were hanging over the side of our tub. Halina's anger at not getting her way channeled itself quite easily to the scissors and Mama's hose. When Mama finally opened the bathroom door, she felt sure her little angel had learned a lesson.

There Halina sat, on the floor, scissors in one hand, finishing her task of cutting up Mama's hose. I could hear Mama's deep intake of breath, but she never said a word. It was only after Tata returned from his morning route a few minutes later that Halina felt the consequences of her terrible deed.

Mama and Tata did not believe in spankings. Their words and a long stare were usually enough to convince us we had better obey or else. Their civil approach to raising a child ended that day with Halina. Tata not only scolded her, but spanked her as well. A spanking that I think hurt my sister's feeling more then the actual slight slaps to her behind. And Mama's scolding afterwards found its mark probably much more accurately then that spanking. Nonetheless, those few slaps my sister received on this day were also painful to me. In a home where love and understanding prevailed every day, it was difficult for me to witness such behavior, not only from my sister, but from my Tata as well. We were a family, and after this I think my sister realized life simply did not center around her. Mama and Tata always reminded us that with all the work they had during the week, there was little time for them to correct foolish behavior on our part.

Mama's world was one of continuity. Babsha had taught her daughters that no matter how poor, poverty was no excuse for lack of cleanliness. Mama not only had the bakery to care for, but the flat upstairs as well. Luckily, while I was a toddler, and for awhile after Halina was born, Mama had Babsha to watch over us and tend to bakery sales as well.

Mama was a typical working mother. Her day began at four-thirty each morning and ended at ten every evening. Each morning she prepared coffee and buttered a slice of bread for Tata before he went out on his route. While he was out, Mama dressed, had her coffee, then went downstairs to prepare the bakery for six A.M. customers.

The front showcases were filled with large cakes; the one inside the store, with sweet rolls. Bread and buns were stalked and lined on the shelves behind the counter. When Tata returned from his route by seven A.M., Mama prepared his breakfast, and many times they sat and enjoyed this meal together.

Tata's breakfast was either a bowl of corn flakes or hot oatmeal, plus a slice of buttered toast with his coffee. On Sunday morning Mama often added a soft boiled egg to his breakfast. Tata never drank his coffee without either a slice of bread and butter, or perhaps a sweet roll.

Floors in the bakers area were scrubbed once a week by Mama. They were mopped daily by Tata; and later, by one of his helpers. The floor in the selling area and the small kitchen were mopped by Mama every evening…and scrubbed thoroughly every Thursday.

The bakery shop opened at six A.M. every morning, six days a week. Until I grew old enough to help, Mama, Tata, and occasionally Babsha, were the only clerks in our bakery.

Monday was laundry day; Tuesday, ironing. Wednesday was Mama's day for shopping, which she usually tried to do in the afternoon. On Thursday she did the downstairs floor scrubbing, and every Friday was devoted to cleaning the flat upstairs. Until Tata bought our first electric sweeper, rugs were swept daily. And of course, there was everything else in between. The sidewalk and gutter were swept each morning, which Tata and Mama at times did together. Except during inclement weather, the sidewalk was always hosed down, Tata's tree and the small plot of grass watered.

Once a month the lace paneled curtains came down. They were washed by hand, starched and hung in the attic on the special stretcher. Windows and blinds were washed before any curtains went back up. I found it interesting how Mama sat on the sill, with half her body hanging out so she could wash the windows on the outside of this second story flat. It seemed there was always something to do and some place to go…cooking, shopping, cleaning.

'When Tata finally bought a rug for the living and dining areas it was just about the time you began to crawl.' Mama did not have to remind me. I remember how marvelous it felt to sit on that rug with Babsha while I played with my doll.

During the week, when Mama was so very busy in the bakery, it was Babsha who helped me wash and dress each morning. Because she knew or spoke so very, very little English, it was from her I learned the Polish language. Her voice was soft and quiet, her smile as constant as a morning sunrise. She kept her dark wavy hair combed back in a soft bun. Her delicate sculptured face was amazingly free of wrinkles. The dresses she wore, except for a removable lace collar around the neck, were dark and plain…mostly brown or black.

Once I began walking greater distances, our day was always the same: rise, wash, dress and go downstairs to greet my parents. In that little kitchen we would join Mama and Tata for breakfast. Then my Babsha and I would go for our morning walk.

Those walks began when I was about two years old. Slowly, to be sure, for my short legs could hardly go too fast. Babsha did not mind. She enjoyed stopping and chatting with neighbors outdoors sweeping their sidewalk or watering their lawn, or repairing their home. In this Polish/Czech neighborhood, Babsha had no trouble at all conversing.

Our trips to Sherman Park and Milwaukee Avenue began just before Halina was born. Visits to the park were glorious. The little lagoon in the center of this park was filled with geese. An island in the center of the lagoon was connected to the park's periphery by three bridges. Curved in a half circle, I loved running up and down each bridge, and squealed with delight as I ran up one side and down the other. Babsha ever vigilant, walking behind me, calling out: 'powolny, moja droga'. Which translated: 'slowly my darling'. There on the island the geese waited for us and the dry bread we brought along for them.

At that young age I never realized how very lucky I was. The great depression began with the collapse of the stock market in 1929. With the bakery his only ever investment, Tata had little to worry about. Somehow his business withstood the test of this difficult period. But he never forgot that others were not as fortunate. Day old bread and rolls were put in large burlap bags at the end of each day. For those who were hungry or not employed, our bakery was open to them. Each morning Mama emptied those burlap bags as she passed out free bakery goods.

When Halina was born in 1931, over eight hundred banks were now closed nationwide. A tall building, called the Empire State, opened in New York. The wealthiest man in Chicago was convicted of tax evasion and sentenced to eleven years in prison.

I felt quite grown-up at four years of age. My excursions with Babsha now included trolley rides to the thickly populated Polish sector on Milwaukee Avenue. The magnificent ethnic stores of Poles and Polish-Jews held a bevy of mouth watering imported goods. Hard and fruit sweet candy, the little gems were filled with rich chocolate; thin wafer delights with thick honey sandwiched between were also a rare treat. But it was the delectable soft sweet candy made from sesame seed, called Halavah, that enticed me the most. Babsha always bought this delightful treat in a little Jewish store. Baked in a large circular form, vanilla flavored or chocolate, the store keeper would slice off a piece, weigh it, then wrap it in brown paper. As we strolled along Milwaukee Avenue, Babsha and I nibbled on small pieces of our Halavah.

It was during one of our trips to this north side area that Babsha took me to my first movie...a Polish movie. My first introduction to a movie, and I was hooked for life. And when she took me to see my first live opera, Carmen, which played on stage at a small theatre, the costumes in this opera entranced me more then the music...which was very lovely but difficult to understand for a small child.

Sunday would always be family day. Because of the hours he spent in the bakery, baking and preparing for his morning route, Tata missed eating evening meals with us. On Sunday Mama made-up for that loss by preparing a large meal that we enjoyed together as a family.

Every Saturday, either Tata or Mama went shopping for a fresh, live chicken. The poultry shop, on 49th and Ashland, sold all sorts of poultry: chicken, geese, duck...most were live. We bought ours live and every Saturday morning it was Babsha's job to chop off that chickens head, pluck its feathers, clean it out, dunk it in boiling water and pluck some more. I learned at an early age what it meant when someone said 'you are running around like a chicken with its head cut off.' Which was exactly what that chicken did after Babsha chopped its head off.

Tata and Mama slept later on Sunday mornings. Still, they were usually awake by seven. Once breakfast ended, Tata retired to the living room with his Polish paper, and Mama pulled out a large pot for the chicken soup she would make that day. After filling the pot with water, in went the cleaned fresh chicken. Next she peeled a large onion and placed it on top a lit burner, next to the pot . The smell of that onion browning permeated the entire flat with its sweet scent. Then into the pot it went with a bouquet of parsley and celery, plus a large bunch of clean carrots, sliced lengthwise, salt and whole peppers. A few bay leaves added to the magnificent scent. Mama then covered this magical soup, brought it to a boil, turned down the flame and let the soup simmer for an hour. Babsha, in the mean time, was busy at the kitchen table mixing and rolling and slicing home-made noodles, ready to dry and then boil up for our early afternoon meal.

Food and family togetherness played an important role in my childhood, as it did for most families in our neighborhood. Both were held in high esteem. I would compare talking about food and enjoying it like one might a great novel that was interesting and delightful to read. Food could never be a hush-hush subject like some forbidden novel that stayed hidden from the world. Mama loved to cook and bake. She watched with utter delight as her skills were consumed with the gusto of a child enjoying the taste of his first piece of chocolate or an ice cream cone. How lucky for her that Tata loved to eat.

Mama's cooking stayed Polish-European for many years. Even after she began cooking such food as Chop Suey and Spaghetti, hers seemed to have a certain touch of Polish in it. Always addicted to lots of onion in her cooking, her Chop Suey was fragrantly sweet with it. When she added a bit of dill to her version of Spaghetti, we accepted the delightful taste readily. Regardless, all her cooking was exceptional. That golden broth with tender pieces of carrots floating among the strands of perfect noodles, our meals were unwitting gourmet delights. Especially a soup called Czernina.

It was a soup one might not eat if the ingredients were revealed. Yet to taste it without knowing those contents is akin to the enjoyment of committing a sin without knowing it is a sin. I would say this is the sweetest most unusual soup ever concocted by the Polish people. Lusciously dark and full of black raisins and purple plums, one eats this soup with light, airy drop dumplings. From the day I fully understand what Mama was cooking, I knew the base of this soup was derived from duck blood. Yes, enough to make people cringe. But when one is introduced to it at an early age, it becomes part of every day life. When Tata brought home a jar of duck blood from the poultry store, I thought nothing of it. Back then I enjoyed the sweetness and richness of this unusual soup. Now...I might think twice before dipping my spoon into this robust meal.

Mama's cooking went in all directions. No doubt most of her choices were influenced by what Tata ate as a young man in Poland. But most of it came from Babsha's teachings.

The menus varied from kidney stew, to fried brains to pickled pigs feet and ox-tail soup. Whatever Mama cooked, there was nothing like coming in from a fall or winter stroll with Babsha and the scent of extraordinary spices wafting down as far as the back porch. In the spring and summer, when all the windows were thrown open for fresh air, Mr. Kreml would often stop us at the little fence that separated our gangway from his back yard and say: 'ah, I can smell a wonderful meal coming from your kitchen today.'

He spoke in Czech to Babsha, she would translate in Polish to me. Later, she made sure to take a bowl or plateful of whatever Mama had cooked. In return, Babsha always received a lovely bouquet of flowers from his garden.

Our kitchen, eventually the entire flat, grew hot on those summer days when the humidity and heat soared through the city. In our area we also had to contend with the stockyard smell when the windows were open. I refused to allow my stomach to give in to the presence of such a fiend. I became rather used to that odor, and like everyone else, found little trouble sitting down and enjoying Mama's cooking.

We were a family of hearty eaters. In between meals only fruits and hard candy was allowed. Mama always made sure she picked the finest selections of vegetables and fruits from a vendors wagon. When he came by each morning, yelling out his arrival, our quiet street gave in to the sound of his voice and the clip-clop of his horses hooves. Later, when he bought his first truck, the honk of his horn became a distinctive call to his arrival.

This was not a neighborhood where people slept late. Men woke very early to get off to work. When the bell tolled six A.M. in St. Augustine's church tower, many women were already outdoors sweeping the gutter and walkway, or shoveling snow in the winter. A variety of vendors already calling out their wares.

Children still in bed had little inclination to sleep late in the spring or summer. It was only during late fall and winter months that a sleeping body found some measure of solitude. With a Chicago wind howling outdoors, the temperature dipping below zero, ice crackling on the windows, radiators hissing indoors, I often turned in bed for a second wink of extra sleep. Beneath that thick fluffy quilt Babsha kept on her bed, the thought of stepping out from beneath it unto a cold floor was more then a reasonable excuse to linger longer in bed.

My memories are filled with the various vendors that graced our neighborhood: the waffle vendor who sold crisp golden waffles sprinkled with powdered sugar. He made those waffles over a fire on a special form…the aroma tingled in my nose, my taste buds watering until he handed me a waffle sitting atop white wrapping paper. It was magical.

All the vendors worked their magic…candy apples— cinnamon flavored hard red candy covered apples that were crisp and rather tart. What could be better on a lazy summer afternoon. Ah, but the evening…that was the time for Sam. Sam the sausage man. The most prolific of all vendors.

Sam was very young when he began his vending operation. Tall, slim, with black hair and eyes to match, he grew old with our neighborhood. When Sam finally did retire, he was bent and gray. But his voice kept that robust sound as he rounded the corner by Slatky's and announced to everyone: 'Sausage-tamales-beef patties'…over and over like a litany to our taste buds. Of course, we knew he was coming before he rounded that corner. The scent of those plump steaming sausages and tamales, the fresh onions and steaming buns…those heavenly beef patties, spiced just right. All kept piping hot in little steamers attached to his vending wagon. Watching Sam put together a sausage link on a long bun, or a beef patty on a round one, slice an onion or open a tamale, was like watching a ballet. Every move was perfection.

Sitting outdoors on those warm summer evenings, Tata and Babsha enjoying their beer, the neighborhood children waiting patiently for Sam, the rhythmic music from Koczubowski's tavern---this was as perfect as any evening could get. Mama preferred a glass of tea with some ice that Tata chipped off the block in our ice box. As I sat next to Babsha on the stoop the led to our bakery, she in one of the three chairs Tata dragged out from indoors, the glass of beer she held in her hand made my mouth water. With hardly a breeze on many hot evenings, that glass dripped more sweat then I did. I imagined how divine that cold liquid must feel going down Babsha's warm throat. Often she would turn to me and smile. Then I knew she was about to offer me a sip. Oh how heavenly! I had been right. But only because Babsha always put two teaspoons of sugar in her beer. Only later, when I tasted some of Tata's left over beer did I discover its true bitterness. After that my love for this amber liquid wearied. For by then, my beloved Babsha was no longer around to tempt me with hers.

Yes, Tata was not only a confirmed eater of hearty food, a good cup of coffee, with a slice of bread of course, a couple of beers in the evening, he also relaxed throughout the day with many strong unfiltered cigarettes. Tata was a slim man when he married Mama; his body changed from slim to solid robust in no time at all.

Mama had a tendency to gain weight as well. Of course she was never very slim. Her weight at marriage was one hundred and twenty-five pounds. Not bad for her five foot four height. After giving birth to Halina, Mama topped the scale at one hundred and eighty pounds. Her busy schedule soon got rid of most of that weight, but until she reached her seventies, her figure was true Reubenesque at one hundred and fifty pounds.

After Halina's birth Mama was busier then ever. Babsha tended to my sister and now I would spend more time with Mama in the bakery. Yet as busy as both my parents continued to be they always had time for us every evening and every weekend. Every other Saturday they continued to visit with close friends, either at our home or their friends home. All other Saturdays and every Sunday belonged to family.

During many of those velvet summer evenings we would take a walk to the small ice cream parlor located on 50th and Ashland. Mama's favorite was always one scoop of vanilla ice cream with fudge topping, whip cream topped with a cherry. But I think she especially enjoyed the four Nabisco wafers that came with this sundae. Tata preferred ice cream sodas. Halina, Babsha and I picked whatever suited us best that evening.

Almost every Sunday Tata drove us to Jackson Park. There we would sit on a grassy knoll and enjoy the cool breeze off of Lake Michigan. Later, during my early school years, when the Good Humor truck was introduced to us, we were treated to an ice cream bar. Each time we hoped to be lucky enough to get a stick that read: 'you get a free ice cream bar.'

Our excursions to the Indiana Sand Dunes came at least twice during a summer. A rather long drive, we would leave early Sunday morning and return just as the bright sun was departing on one end of the sky, the moon appearing on the other. Only one or two times do I remember going to the dunes on a Saturday evening, renting a cabin and sleeping there overnight.

When late fall arrived and during wicked winter weather, I found other things to occupy my time. Paper dolls were always more appealing to me then any other toy.

Even after starting school, and the discovery of reading, I continued in playing with and enjoying those paper dolls...mostly because I liked drawing and designing new clothes for them. It was much like buying new clothes for my own little family.

Spending time in the bakery with Mama each day also became another favorite pastime time of any day and any season. I not only had a chance to watch the bakers perform their miracles with dough in that large oven, I also helped Mama rearrange the inside showcase.

This case was filled with ambrosial bismarks, donuts and small sweet rolls with cheese and various jam fillings that made my mouth water. And since they sold quickly during the morning hours, Mama allowed me to rearrange that case. The golden crisp crusted buns and bread displayed behind the counter sold steadily throughout the day, and I enjoyed watching Mama wrap and bag each item as she chatted away with every customer. Hearing the bell of the cash register each time she punched in a sale, I could hardly wait until that day I became old enough to help her clerk. That would not begin until I reached age nine. For now, I was content with my little job.

We had a dog by the name of Berek, which means Bear in Polish. He and I would sit on Kreml's steps during those days that Mama was too busy in the bakery and Babsha was caring for Halina. With Berek at my feet, we sat and watched people stop to gaze at the cakes in the front showcase. Some went inside to purchase the enticing goods. But these were the depression years, so if anyone did go inside the bakery, it was more for the free day old goods. Tata finally had to cut back on baking so many large cakes. Switching over to baking more of the smaller sweet rolls meant there would be more left over bakery for the poor and hungry.

During the winter months, after what seemed like hours bundling in a snowsuit and clumsy boots, I pulled my sled outdoors and found Rosemary or Clement to play with. Even during these hard times, we had no reason to fear the poor or hungry or those out of work. Clement enjoyed trekking over to the viaduct on the next block and climbing to the top of the hill near the tracks. Sometimes a hobo would be sitting there, waiting for the next freight car to come by, perhaps slow down a bit so he could jump aboard. I remember one hobo, a young man that reminded me so of my Uncle Janek…handsome, a dark mustache…the hobo was dressed in worn clothing. He looked so lost and lonely sitting near those tracks. When Clement asked him to give a push to the sled, the hobo obliged with a sad smile. Perhaps he was remembering his childhood days. Better days, when he was not so hungry and poor. I ran home to get some bread and sweet rolls for him, but by the time I returned, the hobo was gone. Only Clements shouts of laughter filled the air. I always thought him foolish to venture so close to the tracks. The closest I would ever come to climbing to the top of a viaduct was when I was a freshman in high school. That came out of necessity not daring. The viaduct was flooded and we had to climb over the tracks to get to school.

TWO VERY MEMORABLE YEARS

'Brother Can You Spare A Dime', a popular song in 1932, reflected the times as Roosevelt was elected president of the United States. The depression was at its peak. Tata too felt its trickle-down affect. Mama often frequented the new little grocery store that sat in the middle of the block on 49th Place. This grocer opened his doors every morning at five A.M.. Since Tata delivered his bakery goods here, Mama taught it only fitting to trade at his store for most of her groceries. Now with the depression at its very worst, while some of the other grocers cancelled Tata's bakery deliveries, this one continued giving Tata daily orders. Although we were never as hard pressed as those thirteen million Americans that were unemployed, Mama now had to charge the groceries she bought on a day to day basis.

She carried a six by four brown paper bag with her each time she went grocery shopping. When she finished her selection of groceries for the day, Mr. Kopack, the owner of this grocery store, pulled a pencil from behind her ear, wet the tip on his tongue, then proceeded to write down the amount of each item on the brown bag. At the end of each week he totaled the amount and Mama paid what she owed.

'During that rather meager period I went back to making a big pot of soup from one large beef bone. Thankfully Tata enjoyed simple meals. He filled up easily on soup and bread...bread I often spread with bacon grease from the bacon I fried from time to time to accompany his eggs. He never complained. There were so many others in much worse shape then we were. Tata knew how to relax with his Polish paper and his friends. When they came to visit, they seemed to have so much to talk about.' This Mama told me when we talked about those depression years.

Tata and his friends no doubt talked about such things as the kidnapping of Charles Lindbergs infant son, or wondering if Roosevelt would be more successful in healing our country. And of course, hoping to have Prohibition repealed. 'Which I almost hated to see happen,' Mama said, 'now Tata had cut down so much on drinking beer…which I felt was better for his health.'

Mama also added she would always remember that Christmas of '32 as one of everyone having high hopes that things would begin to improve in '33. Later, it would be remembered as I only remember it: this was Babsha's final Christmas with us.

In '33 Roosevelt's 'New Deal' did create many new jobs. But not enough to stop a madman from trying to assassinate the president. 'Too many people are still starving' was the madman's reasoning for the attempt. The bullet missed its mark. It hit Anton Cermak, the mayor of Chicago, and killed him.

This same year, another madman by the name of Hitler assumed power in Germany.

'Our bakery sales finally took an upward turn in '33.' Tata told me proudly in recalling that time in stories of the past. 'Thankfully so.' Mama added, 'Babsha was more anxious then ever to take a trip to Poland.

'You were close to five years old now,' Mama continued, 'it was in 1932, on an early November morning when Babsha first mentioned her desires. I remember it so well. Halina was sitting in her high chair, Babsha feeding her oatmeal. I was brushing your hair.' Which, if I recall correctly, was not a complicated chore. My reddish-blond hair was thick and always kept in a short bob. It may have had a little natural curl when I was an infant, but now only the body remained. 'It was a quiet Sunday morning,' Mama said, 'With a touch of autumn in the air. The windows were wide open in the kitchen bedroom, the air fresh and free of stockyard stench for a change. Tata was sitting at the table drinking coffee and enjoying a slice of toast and jam. Babsha's request came as a big surprise.

"Would it be possible" 'she asked, "for me to visit Czestochowa…to see my husband's grave…that place where your Papa is buried." A question asked so simply and easily, yet it troubled my mind. All I could do was look to your Tata. Without blinking an eye he nodded. He adored Babsha, and would go to the ends of the earth for her.'

'Somehow,' Tata told me years later, 'We found the means to grant her this wish.'

So our Christmas Eve celebration in 1932 would be planned as a going away feast for Babsha's upcoming trip to Poland in 1933. Little did Mama, or any of us realize, how prophetic this good-bye gift would be. Mama of course was planning a bigger celebration for the following Eve in '33, when Babsha would be home again from her trip to Poland.

Our lives went on as usual the rest of that year in '32. Walks through the park, around the block, one or two trips to Milwaukee Avenue to purchase special Christmas candy. All came with a lightness in Babsha's step now, perhaps likened to someone about to relive their past again…that anxious joy one feels at just the thought.

We exchanged more visits with Aunt Isabelle and Uncle George until that Eve, when everyone would gather at our house. My cousin Eddie was about ten years old now and growing taller it seemed with each visit. Alfreda, who was two years older, showed early on the beauty she would possess one day. Yet it is from later years that I remember my two older cousins the best: Eddie, so handsome in his army uniform and married to Violet. The sadness I felt when he died of cancer in his early fifties. Tall and beautiful Alfreda, with her sultry voice and dimpled cheeks, was always the epitome of fashion. I remember one outfit she wore with great clarity. A blue-gray suit, trimmed in dark gray fur at neck and cuffs, tiny buttons running down from neck to waist, the outfit was made for her tall slim figure with perfection. She visited with us often, taking time to do so on her way home from work as a secretary in a downtown office. It was there she met and married Elmer Rasmussen, a rather wealthy business man. After that, Alfreda lived in one of Chicago's' more opulent suburbs. It was only after she and Elmer moved to Tucson, in the seventies, that I talked to her again. Even though we only visited via phone, we had some memorable talks. When Elmer phoned me one day to let me know Alfreda had died of a heart attack it shocked me. She was only fifty-six years old. She always told Elmer she would die exactly as Babsha did, and at the same age.

I had always been close to my two younger cousins, Herby and Madalaine, even more so in 1933. We were closer in age, so it was probably a given that we had more in common then I found with Eddie or Alfreda. It would be only after Aunt Isabelle and Uncle George decided to move to California that I lost touch with them. Then Madalaine got married and settled in California. By the time Herby returned to Chicago, I was married and living in another state. Herby died of cancer in 1998.

But without any doubt, that Christmas Eve of 1932 will always bring happy memories, as will most of 1933. I often wish I could relive that last Eve with Babsha. Mama went all out with her cooking that year and Babsha helped in the kitchen like a young woman anticipating something wondrous about to happen.

According to Polish tradition, Wigilia, or the Eve of Christmas, is the day of big celebration. A day of abstinence, Mama knew how to make a feast out of this meatless day. For Tata, who's religion only went as far as living by the golden rule, followed this meatless tradition with gusto. Surprisingly, he did the same on Good Friday and Holy Saturday as well. His faith in God, I always knew, far exceeded his faith in organized religion.

Mama's menu on this eve would also exceed our Eve's of the past. The variety of fish would be greater, more poppy seed in her buttered noodles, and not only did she cook up a vegetarian soup made from dry imported mushrooms, she also served a vegetarian borsch.

The hearty tender dumplings she made, called pierogi, would be filled this year not only with saurkraut or cheese, but also with mashed potatoes. The hearty and tender little dumplings would look glorious swimming on top the ruby-red broth. Tata's favorite was always a jar of pickled herring with a side dish of boiled potatoes. This was his appetizer before our big meal. Everything in our home this year seemed decorated more brightly and deliciously then ever before…both edibly and ornamentally.

We always had a live tree. We walked to the Christmas tree vendor, which was located on Ashland Avenue, about two days before the eve. Tata picked the tree out by himself when I was too young to accompany him. It was after Halina was born that I was finally allowed the pleasure of joining Tata on his quest. His challenge was not only to find the fullest, greenest tree, but the least expensive one as well.

Whether it was something he learned as a young man in Poland or after he arrived in America, when he had to count every penny earned and spent, Tata had a knack for getting a sales man to lower the cost of just about anything. Tata called this trait 'Jewing down the price'. He not only did it with our yearly Christmas tree, but with other purchases as well: cars, furniture, even clothing. I remember all too clearly when he took me along to Maxwell Street on a Sunday shopping spree. I was about twelve years old at the time.

The Jews that lived on Maxell Street were Russo-Polish Jews. The women wore shawls and the men had long beards and wore long black coats. For Tata, who came from that part of Poland under Russian rule, he found little trouble communicating with the people in this part of Chicago. During this time I was in need of a new winter coat and a pair of shoes. Tata assured me I would find exactly what I was hoping for in this shopping district.

Quite happily Tata allowed me to choose a lovely red coat lined and trimmed in faux leopard fur. I felt a little foolish when he began haggling with the salesman on the price of this coat, for I did not think it was that expensive to begin with. But, both men finally reached an agreeable price and now I looked forward to my new shoes. Unfortunately, I did not do as well with this choice. We disagreed on what I hoped for and what Tata thought was a better suited pair of sturdy shoes for all the walking I did . Besides, the shoes I chose were much more expensive then those Tata chose…and the salesman refused to lower the cost to suit Tata. It was then the 'sturdy pair' caught Tata's eye. I cringed. He haggled, and won. I told Tata, at least outwardly, that I was content with the shoes, and said, to please him, that this was a much better pair. Inwardly, they reminded me of the shoes Miss Slatky wore—tied up the front with a one and a half inch heel, black…I immediately dubbed them 'old maid' shoes. Yet, how could I refuse? Children did not argue with their parents, nor voice many strong opinions, especially in front of strangers.

I wore my coat with great pride. After wearing the shoes only once, I hid them in the kitchen closet behind Mama's shoes, and told Mama they were just too uncomfortable to wear. Wise as always, Mama guessed the real reason for my not wearing the old maid shoes. While washing the closet floor one day, I noticed they were gone. I asked Mama what had happened to them. 'Well, Emily's mother needed a pair of shoes. They were just her size and she was so happy to get them. I knew you would not mind my giving them away, since they hurt your feet.' I smiled and gave her a hug of gratitude. The following week I went shopping on Ashland with Mama and found the perfect pair of shoes at Meyers Department Store.

Tata always seemed to find that perfect Christmas tree. Full of not, after Mama finished decorating it, our tree always looked fit for a king. We always decorated our tree the day before Christmas Eve. It sat in a corner of our living where it could be seen as soon as one stepped into the dining area. Decorated with strings of large electric bulbs and all sorts of sweets, Halina and I helped with the decorations when we were just barely walking. Ginger cookies that were baked in shapes of angels and Santas, each had a glazed paper print glued to the front depicting the form. These were saved from year to year, and tucked away with all of Mama's other fancy ornaments of silver and gold, and all trimmed in white frosted paint. Miniature chocolate bottles, filled with a variety of liquors and wrapped in intensely bright foil, hung alongside each cookie. This candy, which was purchased at any ethnic shop on Ashland Avenue or Milwaukee Avenue, was passed out to everyone on Christmas Day and consumed quite anxiously. The tree glittered shamelessly, not only in the evening among the lit bulbs, but on those days when sunlight swam into our living room, and wrapped itself around our richly decorated tree.

The bottom of our tree was covered with a white bed sheet. On this Mama arranged a tiny village of houses and churches made of papier-mache, each painted colorfully, and each with sparkling white paint on the roof that looked like snow. Mama made sure each little building had one bulb inside. With our living room lights off in the evening, only the tree lights sparkling, the village came to life like a picture post card. Circling around the village, a little wood fence sparkled white and bright around the winter scene.

It was during advent, those days before Christmas Eve arrived, that Babsha always prepared her fresh Polish sausage. I always accompanied her to the Polish butcher shop on Ashland and watched and listened as she purchased the meat that would go into the casing of that sausage.

Downstairs in the bakers area sat a separate table, about six feet long and four feet wide, it was used as a work area for everything from filling fresh deep fried bismarks to lining up Tata's freshly baked Easter lambs...and during Advent, for Babsha as she prepared her sausage.

Tata had special manual equipment for both the bismark filling and the sausage stuffing. For the bismarks all he had to do was fill one end of the machine with strawberry or prune jam. On the other end was a long narrow tip, to which he pierced each light, dark golden bismark. Holding it carefully with one hand, Tata pumped a handle with the other hand, until, magically the machine filled each little round cake with jam.

The contraption Babsha used for making sausage seemed a bit more complicated. First she had to ground up all of the raw meat she purchased from the butcher shop. Into a hand grinder would go pork, beef and veal. After adding all her special spices, she packed the meat into a wide opening at the top. At the other end a long nozzle was fitted with special casing that would hold the ground meat. Casing fitted, she began to pump a handle, up and down, up and down, until—amazingly—the casing began to expand as it filled with the meat. When she had a piece about twelve inches in length, Babsha then tied off that piece with a bit of string and began the process over again. The entire procedure produced about twelve to fifteen twelve inch links of fresh Polish sausage.

With all its special seasonings, Babsha's sausage had not only mouth watering flavor, the scent as it boiled was astoundingly pungent-sweet. When we were ready to enjoy a meal of this delectable concoction, which was on Christmas Day and later on Easter Sunday, Mama would boil the links for about forty-five minutes to and hour. Then she would put the links in her large iron skillet and brown the pieces in her oven for about half an hour. A truly preservative free meal. Before Tata bought Mama's first refrigerator, all the sausage was cooked on Christmas day, some links wrapped securely and put away in the coldest spot of our ice-box and saved for Easter Sunday.

Mama's finest linens, china, glassware and silverware came out on Christmas Eve. If we had company on Christmas Day, which we often did, considering all the friends my parents had, the china, glassware and silverware that was washed on the Eve was never put away until after Christmas Day. Aunt Isabelle and Uncle George, Uncle Janek and Ciocia Mania, and all my cousins were the only company we had on Christmas Eve. It was a family gathering that continued with Aunt Isabelle and her family even after Babsha's death. Ciocia Mania ceased to visit with us after Uncle Janek died. She seemed to withdraw herself from the world after that.

I found Christmas Day almost as enjoyable as the eve, when Tata and Mama's dearest and closest friends joined us for an early evening meal. Mr. and Mrs. Gongolova and their son Joseph, Mr. Chmielewski, his son Ted and his daughter Zosia, were with us during many Christmas Days. The Gongolova's lived on the north side of Chicago in a third floor apartment. Visiting there was like being at my Ciocia Mania's...those apartments seemed to have their own scent. All the beautifully varnished woodwork, doors and floors had permeated the halls and flats with a clean, sweet woodsy smell.

Mrs. Gongolova was a stately lady with blue-black hair and skin I thought almost as white as snow. She kept her back so straight and stiff I often wondered how she ever married Mr. Gongolova, who was shorter, stocky, and a most outgoing man—full of laughter and songs. He also did all of the cooking for his family. Whenever our meals were over on Christmas Day, it was he who volunteered to clear the table and wash the dishes. He was truly adored by everyone in this crowd, perhaps more then by Mrs. Gongolova, who, by Mama's account, had her eye on Tata. 'I always had to watch her. And I never let Tata out of my sight when she was around.'

Their son Joseph was another story. I could never figure him out, he was so withdrawn and quiet. He wasn't bad looking either, with his mother's dark hair, and dark eyes hiding behind thick dark rimmed glasses. When I found out later he went on to attend the University of Chicago, on a scholarship, I concluded he must have found us very boring.

Mr. Chmielewski was by far Tata's most cherished friend. He visited with Tata often as we did with him. Mr. Chmielewski was also a baker by trade. His bakery was on 55th. and Ashland. His baking forte was exquisite little cookies and poppyseed cake. I never met Mrs. Chmielewski, for unfortunately she had a nervous breakdown before I was born. She was confined to a mental institution. Their son Ted was tall, blond and rather handsome. But also so shy that I hardly got to know him. The only time he seemed more at ease was when Tata took me along to visit at their bakery shop. A very small shop with living quarters in the back. Teddy would bring me a plate of his father's freshly baked cookies or a slice of poppyseed cake. Still, even while we sat nibbling at our treat, our fathers in deep conversation, Ted hardly spoke. His sister Zosia was the most gorgeous of creatures. She had large blue eyes, pearl pink translucent skin, tall and slim and pale blond hair that covered her head like thick strands of silk. I loved watching her as we sat around the dining room table on Christmas Day. She always wore white and reminded me of some sort of a winter snow fairy.

Mama believed in starting Christmas Eve preparations early—as early as six A.M on the morning of the eve.

First, out came the silverware, which she polished to a high shine. Of course, all the furniture and every room had been cleaned the day before. Then out would come her lovely ecru tablecloth and matching napkins, all with exquisitely etched and embroidered corners. She would press each piece before placing them on the dining room table, which by now was expanded to its full length with the two extra inserts. Next, her best china and glowing silverware. The china was a gift from Babsha; the silverware, from Uncle Janek. The special glassware, so clean it reflected every light, would hold Tata's best wine, or liqueur.

That cherry liqueur was also served as a before dinner drink…which made up for the lack of wine during prohibition.

The finished setting on Mama's mahogany table looked stunning and inviting to the eye. I myself could hardly wait until all our company arrived. By noon Mama was busy in the kitchen. The vapors of all the different scents wafted throughout the entire flat. The wait seemed endless. Of course, we all had to bathe and dress properly for this occasion.

This Christmas Eve Mama bought me a bright blue velvet dress with a white lace collar, and patent leather shoes. Halina had a duplicate of this dress, only hers was red. After Mama brushed our hair and put a small matching ribbon into it, I felt as decked out as our Christmas tree.

Now came the finishing touches to our splendid feast: A large divided white plate was filled with an assortment of imported hard candies; a smaller wood bowl, its center holding a silver nut cracker and picks, held a variety of nuts. Tata, hardly one to keep his tummy empty and waiting all day for good food, loved to nibble on the nuts. In fact, it was he who cracked the nuts for us as we sat around our shining tree every evening.

By six o'clock all of our company would have arrived. The men sitting in the living room, enjoying a bit of Tata's liqueur, the women in the kitchen helping Mama and chatting away about how lovely and appetizing everything looked. Babsha, who usually sat at the kitchen table and observed the festivities most Eve's, took a more active part in helping Mama this Christmas Eve.

The children were all excited and very hungry by now. We had to be quieted down and told not to run in and out of the kitchen door, up and down the hall and porch steps. 'You are allowing too much cold air into the kitchen…each time you allow the door to yawn I feel the cold air.' We would settle down with a deep sigh, but soon we would give in to our restless bodies and run about again.

During this Christmas Eve of '32 our home was still full of relatives. They would begin to diminish in a few years time, first Babsha, then Uncle Yanek, followed by Ciocia Mania. The only relative who never joined in our festivities was my uncle the doctor, who before his death at least phoned Tata and wished him 'wesolek swiant', which means happy holiday. Still, regardless of who was there with us or was not, Tata always said: 'all we can do is remember the love they gave us while they were with us. Those are the memories we must keep alive and cherish as we celebrate our holidays. Those we loved that are now gone will stay in our hearts forever.'

As we all sat down to our meat-free meal this Eve, the first tradition on this Christmas Eve meal was to break a white wafer called oplatek. This wafer, about eight by five inches in size, always had an etched holy scene of the Christmas season stamped unto it. The ethnic stores on Ashland Avenue that sold imported goods always carried this during the Christmas season. By tradition it should have been blessed by a priest before being broken and consumed. Whether Mama did so or not she never said. But I do know that years later, when Mama purchased our oplatek from a religious store associated with St. Augustine church, those wafers were all pre-blessed.

Mama and Tata were always the first to break the wafer in half and wish each other love and best wishes. Then each of them went around the table and broke their piece with everyone else seated at the table. If anyone wished to break their piece with someone they could also do so. With all this company, and everyone wanting to wish everyone else special tidings, Mama and Tata usually broke two or three wafers at the onset of this ritual.

After all the solemnity, the chattering and laughter began as we started our fine meal of soup, fish, pierogi, and poppyseed noodles. The sumptuous meal always ended with fresh brewed coffee, a slice of poppyseed cake, either baked by Tata or Mr. Chmielewski. Years later, after our bakery closed, Mama always took to baking her very own luscious poppyseed cake. I always thought hers more ambrosial then Tata's. She added more raisins and nuts to her poppyseed filling. The fresh ground poppyseed she used was purchased in a coffee shop on Ashland Avenue. During the Christmas holiday they also catered to grinding poppyseed. It seemed much tastier then the one Tata purchased in bulk. Regardless, this special dessert rounded out our extraordinary meal quite nicely.

Children under twelve usually drank milk at meals, but on such special occasions we were allowed a cup of half coffee and half milk. Actually, I always preferred milk-tea to coffee. Mama made this for me in a tall glass, always making sure a spoon sat in that glass before she poured the very hot water—which kept the glass from cracking. Then she would add enough cool milk to make the drink lukewarm, plus a heaping teaspoon of sugar or honey. To me this was much tastier and felt more soothing then coffee, which I found rather bitter...despite the addition of any sweetener.

Mama always said sitting around the table for a spell after any meal, conversing and sipping coffee, nibbling on dessert, was a pleasant way to allow our food a good settling. It also seemed to bring family closer together. Conversations never led to any arguments or disagreement. They were kept civil and cheerful, especially when children were involved. I almost hated to see them come to an end, but soon the women began to quietly gather dishes and left over food into the kitchen, where everything was placed on the table. Left-overs were always shared with family and friends to carry home. The remainder went into Mama's green ice-box, the cold pantry, or on the roof next door.. Then while Mama began rinsing and washing all the empty plates and pots, the rest of us took up towels to help dry. With so many helpers, we had everything washed, wiped and put away in no time at all. Now our Christmas Eve festivities were ready to begin.

Until I was about nine or ten years old, Tata always dressed up as Santa Clause. When he was younger and slimmer, Mama said a pillow had to be tucked inside the red pants and coat to depict Santa's big tummy. By the time I was born and then became fully aware of Santa, that tummy was all his own. Since we did not have a fireplace for Santa's well known entrance, Mama said he had to arrive via the gangway after leaving his sled and reindeer on our roof. One day, when Tata apparently forgot to pick up the whip Santa supposedly carried to encourage reindeer speed, I found it the following morning, on Christmas

Day, still resting against the wall in the hallway, next to a now empty bucket, which we filled with water for his thirsty reindeer. How could he forget this, I questioned Mama. 'Oh my goodness...' Mama answered without blinking an eye, 'let me put this out in the gangway. I am sure Santa will pick it up on the way back to the North Pole.' Of course, her explanation sounded logical. It made me believe even more that indeed, our Santa was the real thing.

Our Santa carried a large white bag, (probably once a bag that was filled with the flour Tata used in his bakery) now filled with Christmas gifts. This year I received a Shirley Temple doll: about twelve inches tall, with golden curls and dimpled cheeks, this true image of the little star was beautiful in a blue velvet dress. Halina received a baby doll that cried each time she was turned over. Herby found a red fire engine in his package; Madalaine, a fine new purse with a dollar bill inside. Handkerchiefs, hand tatted by either Babsha or Mama, and new socks were gifts we could expect every Eve. Mama always received a bottle of her favorite perfume...Coty's Emeraude. I loved the delicious scent of this perfume, sweet and woodsy. I could hardly wait until I was old enough to receive my very own bottle. That request was filled when I turned twelve. Of course, by then I also knew who was behind the white beard and full mustache.

The grown-ups were also remembered in a very special way, on Christmas Eve as well as Christmas Day. Everyone received two or three links of Babsha's heavenly Polish sausage and a small bottle of Tata's very own cherry liqueur. The 'Ohs' and 'Ahs' when Santa pulled out links of sausage and Tata's liquor, all covered in special wrappings, never ceased...regardless of how many years this occurrence took place. Babsha's eyes sparkled with delight, and I swear Tata's chest grew bigger each year. Babsha especially enjoyed this holiday and the sharing of all our love and joy.

The Eve celebration was one evening the children got to stay up late. There were Christmas carols to sing, stories to tell, more nuts to crack and of course the time to enjoy our new toys. Most of the carols were sung in Polish. Later, after I started school, I introduced those carols in English, which Mama and Tata enjoyed just as much.

Although we never attended mass on Christmas Day while I was very young, the little manger nestled in the village beneath our tree attested to the fact we never forgot who's birthday we were celebrating. And just as she did every evening before we finally crawled beneath our covers in bed, Mama made sure we knelt down at the side of that bed to say our evening prayers of thanks. My prayers, until I made my first communion, were said in Polish. Later, when I learned those same prayers in English, I knew their meaning was the same in any language.

Mama wanted Halina and me to make our First Holy Communion together. Since one had to be at least seven years old for this religious celebration, and Halina's birthday fell in September, we were allowed to make our first communion in 1939. At ten and a half years of age, I felt very old among those youngsters. But everything worked out splendidly, a month later I wore that same communion outfit of white dress, stockings and shoes, and because I was now old enough, was allowed to participate in being confirmed. Joan, the name I picked after reading about St. Joan of Arc, was added to my name. All of this of course happened long after this well remembered Christmas Eve.

New years Eve would also be Babsha's final time to watch over us while Mama and Tata attended a New Years Eve dance and celebration with their Polish choir of friends.

February and my fifth birthday came as usual. Mama was never very big on birthday celebrations, but she always baked me a cake, decorated it with candles, bought some ice cream and invited my Aunt and Uncle and my cousins for a small party to help celebrate this day. By Polish tradition, people celebrated names day rather then birth days. Mama went with American tradition when it came to our birthdays. Tata, we found out later, was the only one who remembered his names day rather then his birth day.

For years I believed when we celebrated that day in November it was Tata's birthday we were celebrating. Only later, when he showed me his birth certificate, did I realize he was actually born on July 4th. After that marvelous discovery, we always celebrated his birthday on the right day—and always teased him that the entire country was celebrating his birthday!

Following other customs brought from Poland, especially since Babsha was a practicing Midwife there, we hardly ever had any need to see a physician. I remember having a stuffy nose and not feeling too well on my fifth birthday. Easy to recall, since according to Mama I was a healthy child. If Mama even suspected a cold coming on in either of her two children, or Tata for that matter, the camphor oil and flannel cloths would come as quickly as frost on our windows during Chicago's frosty winters. During these times I don't even know if there was such a thing as an emergency room in any hospital…at least I never recall going to one or hearing of people running to one for every little ache and pain or runny nose. Hot tea with lemon and honey was used for a cough. If we coughed too long, a half teaspoon of Tata'' liqueur added to the tea would quickly dispel any tickling in our throat, and certainly help us sleep better at night.

I do remember two periods in my very young life that a severe illness struck both of us. When I came down with a bad case of sore throat, with no help at all from that special tea, Mama did resort to calling Dr. Kalinowski. I feel now this must have been a strep throat, although it was not diagnosed as such. I do remember doing a lot of gargling and having to take daily teaspoons of a nasty tasting medicine, that contained iodine, for about two weeks. Of course, every doctor then made house calls…perhaps this was the emergency room visit coming to a home, rather then the other way around. Which seemed a much better and safer way to treat people. One was never exposed to any other illness while sitting and waiting in an overcrowded emergency room area.

Halina's illness was much more serious. She developed a severe case of whooping cough. Dr. Kalinowski was no longer alive to treat her, and we never had a family doctor. Thankfully Tata remembered his brother talking about a case he handled with the same symptoms my sister now showed. Tata decided to treat Halina's cough just as his brother may have had he been there.

My sister's illness came in the late fall of the year before I began first grade. Babsha was no longer with us, so I followed close to Mama as she cared for Halina. The dry laborious cough that comes with this illness seems to wrack a child small body. Tata finally told Mama one evening to bundle us up, we were going for a ride to Jackson Park. There we would park and sit near the shore of Lake Michigan.

As he asked, Mama bundled us up, and with an extra blanket around Halina, we all crawled into Tata's automobile. Mama in the front, with Halina on her lap, I in the back, feeling cozy beneath the extra blanket we kept back there. When we reached the parking area near Lake Michigan, Tata parked as close as possible to the lake. Then he rolled down his window half way and instructed Mama to do the same. The cold moist air coming off the lake entered our car like fingers searching for warm bodies. For a moment I shivered, and quickly nestled deeper into the wool blanket. Tata explained to Mama that inhaling this moist cold air would help my sister's croup. And indeed, she seemed to be breathing easier. It took at least two or three evenings of this moist air therapy before Halina finally pulled out of the miserable coughing. By then Mama was almost as exhausted as my poor little sister. Tata, in his ever present state of faith, never once surrendered to giving up his belief this therapy would eventually help.

Christmas came and went, and the new year of 1933 began. We all looked forward to spring and Easter. Babsha of course talked of nothing else but planning her visit to Poland. I heard Mama mention once to Tata that she was a bit concerned the trip might be too much for Babsha. 'How could a voyage over that same ocean that holds so many sad memories for her possibly cheer her?' Mama once questioned as she talked with Tata. It was early morning, we were seated at the table in the little downstairs kitchen, finishing our breakfast. Babsha was upstairs tending to Halina. I was eating an apple Tata had peeled and sliced for me. He answered Mama's question before taking his final sip of coffee. 'She has never been to her husband's grave. Her heart yearns to see this. To see the city of her youth…how can we deny her this trip.' As Mama stood to clear off the table, she simply nodded in agreement. Later, when Babsha came downstairs with Halina, to take us for a walk around the block, Mama asked her when she planned on making the trip to Poland. 'In September. Yes, that sounds like a very good month to travel.' Babsha answered as Mama bundled us up to go outdoors.

It was still very chilly outdoors. The ground covered in those confetti traces of snow that told us winter was still determined to stay a bit longer. We could count on our nose and cheeks turning bright pink just after circling the block once. By the time we finished going around at least two more times, Halina in her buggy and I barely ambling along in my snowsuit outfit and galoshes that rendered these morning walks so tiring. There were never too many people out on such days...if there was any sidewalk cleaning to do, most waited until mid-morning, when the temperature went up a bit. On these cold days I could hardly wait until I finally got home to a cup of very warm milk tea and my toys.

It was just before Easter of this year that Mama suddenly decided I join the Settlement House near 47th. and Ashland, where classes were offered in reading and writing our Polish language. Mama said it would be another nice gift to give Babsha before her departure...my learning how to read and write the language of my heritage. To learn any foreign language or hear it in any classroom during these years was as unheard of as any signs or instructions in public places catering to any foreign language. Immigrants had to realize they were Americans now, and they had best learn this countries language if they really wanted to expand their horizons. But, as many immigrants felt, one cannot forget ones roots. So the week-end alternative to learn more Polish seemed a logical step in Mama's mind. No doubt more so then in mine...although now I wish I had been as eager as she.

Regrettably, I enjoyed dancing the Krakowiak more then learning the reading or writing of my inherited language. This Polish dance is exhilarating, to say the least. Surprisingly, it was Babsha who was just as excited as me about the dance, I was about to learn on those week-ends. Her heart, I believe to this day, was still back in Poland, no matter how much she believed her migration to America had been the best move. Her thoughts forever stayed with the man and country she loved. When she revealed to me how much she loved dancing the Polka with her husband when she was that young girl back in Poland it took away any guilt I felt relishing the dancing more then the studying the art of writing and reading Polish. And when the time came to prepare my costume for a special recital of Polish dancing, it was Babsha who volunteered her sewing skills instantly.

As Babsha sewed the pieces together of my white peasant blouse and calf length white skirt, I wonder now what her thoughts were. Was she remembering the hills of Poland? As she trimmed that skirt with pastel colored ribbon, did she hear the peasants, that lived on those hills, singing, and in her mind did she see them dancing? I know how painstaking the time it took to sew everything together, especially that red velvet vest that had streamers of red and white ribbon attached to one shoulder. Every evening, as I lay in bed, I could hear the sound of that pedal on Mama's sewing machine going clap-clap-clap as Babsha sewed on to early morning. My eyes grew heavy as the synchronized sound engulfed my thoughts. The rhythm stopping every now and then, and starting again as my mind drifted off into sound sleep. I felt as excited as Babsha when my costume was at last complete.

The red vest, lined in red taffeta, was covered on its entire front and back with sparkling sequins in various glittering tones and designs of leaves and flowers. Sewn on entirely by hand, it was a work of art. The finished piece so dazzling and beautiful I felt the loveliest creature that Saturday afternoon of our recital at the Settlement House. As I danced in a circle with the children of that Polish class, the tapping of our tambourines and the music of Poland filled the room. Skirts whirling around our legs, the red and white ribbons, colors of the Polish flag, trailed behind us as we danced ever so proudly. My cheeks felt flushed. I am sure they were as pink as the band of flowers in my hair.

I looked over at Babsha as our circle of dancers stopped for a second to sing. The smile on her face, the sparkle in her eyes, the glow on her cheeks made her look so young and beautiful at that moment. Surely she was back in Poland, a young girl again. A young woman in love. Her urge to return no doubt much stronger now then ever. Or perhaps, a feeling that the time had come to join her beloved husband as well.

My lessons at the settlement ended with that recital. Easter was just around the corner. A very busy time for Tata and Mama, plus, I am quite sure they realized my heart was not really into learning to read and write the Polish language. The one thing I would regret in later years. For now, Mama seemed content that I at least knew and understood the Polish language…enough to converse with Tata and Babsha.

Easter of '33, as any other Easter, was a busy holiday for the bakery shop. So many special treats had to be baked for this day. Everything according to Polish custom: small loaves of rye bread with a cross indentation in the center and Easter lamb cakes, each one colorfully decorated. Dozens of each were baked to be ready for Holy Week. This year, with more people back at work, the orders seemed to double. Mama always helped with the lamb cakes, but this year Tata had to hire extra help for the preparation of dough.

His name was Miecheck, Tata's new baker. He was short, slim and as much as I always thought Tata always a happy cheerful person, Miecheks singing and whistling was non-stop. When he mixed, when he pounded or rolled…no matter what he was doing, Miechecks energy seemed boundless. Or perhaps it only looked that way next to Tata's deliberate slow and easy manner. Regardless, Miecheck took over much of the mixing and baking—except for the lambs. They were Tata's specialty.

A relatively simple pound cake mix, perhaps the mixture of lard and butter gave this sweet dense pound cake so much flavor. Mama, however, always insisted on adding a little more rum flavoring then usual, so no doubt it also added much to the delightful taste of this cake. I was always amazed how perfect every single lamb came out of its mold. All that mixing, all that batter, and never any errors.

While Tata mixed, Mama greased the special iron lamb forms, which consisted of two pieces—top and bottom. The batter, thick and yellow and creamy as butter, was spooned into the bottom half of each small or large mold. Then the other half, with a little hole in the middle that allowed steam to escape, was placed on top. The lamb mold was actually lying on its back. Each mold was then placed into the large brick oven and baked for about forty-five minutes to an hour. When Mama pulled a few molds out of the oven, she always tested the cake through that little hole at the top with a straw plucked from a broom and washed for testing. If the straw came out free of dough, the lambs were ready to pull out of the oven and set on the large butcher block table to cool.

Once cooled, Mama would pry open the top half and gently release the lamb from the bottom half by running a knife along the edge, then carefully turning it over—and like a miracle of birth, there it stood, a perfectly shaped lamb cake…all golden brown and regal. By the time all the lambs were baked and cooled, not only was this butcher block table covered with lambs, but the long table against the wall as well. Now the kitchen table had to be completely cleared off. Tata would sit here and begin his expertise decoration of each lamb.

Tata prepared the luscious white frosting in four separate bowls. One mix stayed pure white; to another he added yellow food coloring, to the next pink and to the last green. Filling a cloth bag with the white frosting first, Tata covered each lamb with swirls and twirls that looked like lambs wool when finished. With the colored frosting he added flowers and leaves. Each lamb sat on a bed of thick cardboard, for easier handling. The final touch in Tata's decorating was a skirt of green frosting around the bottom of each lamb. Now Mama's turn came to give each lamb a final touch of decorating.

She used cloves for the eyes; a toothpick dipped in red food coloring became a strip of mouth across the white frosting. Mama tied a small red ribbon around the neck of each lamb. 'The little lambs signify Christ as the Lamb of God, the red ribbon around each neck is the blood He lost for our sins.' Then she proceeded to make up little red and white flags that were glued to toothpicks. They were inserted atop the lambs back. Since Tata's bakery catered to a mostly Polish populace, the flag signified Polish tradition. Of course it could easily be removed for any other customer. Everything, the baking, the decorating, had to be completed before Holy Week. The lambs were always sold by Good Friday. According to Polish tradition, a small portion of each food to be eaten on Easter Sunday, had to be blessed on Holy Saturday.

Mama prepared such baskets for us when Halina and I grew old enough to walk to St. John of God Church. Each basket contained a very small loaf of rye bread, a few hard boiled and decorated eggs, butter in the shape of a lamb, Polish sausage, a piece of lamb cake, a few slices of ham, horseradish, salt, and candy. We stayed away from eating candy during Lent. On Easter Sunday I was always more anxious to get at that then any of the other food.

Each basket was covered with a dainty linen cloth that had been tatted colorfully on its edges by either Mama or Babsha. Many other people that we met on the way to Easter food blessing on Holy Saturday carried very similar baskets. Children, young women and very old women, seldom any men, all headed toward the courtyard of that same church.

We all waited patiently for that half hour before the priest came out of the church vestibule. I knew most of the people who gathered here on this day. Most bought bakery at Tata's shop. Many I knew from trips with Mama to Ashland shopping, or walks with Babsha around the block. I felt great pride seeing Tata's delicate work displayed so proudly in most of those baskets.

Finally, dressed in full vestment and holding his sprinkler, called an asperge, an altar boy at his side carrying a silver bucket filled with holy water, the priest stepped out into the crowd of people. Everything grew quiet, the talking and laughter ceased. The priest greeted us with a smile and instructed us to uncover our baskets and raise them as high as possible. After saying a few prayers, he dipped the asperge in the bucket of holy water, he raised it high above his head and with swift flips of his wrist and moving his arm from side to side, he sprinkled holy water across and unto the crowd.

I could feel the water dance on my face as he shook the sprinkler across everyone and continued with his prayers of blessing. He then wished everyone a happy and blessed Easter before turning back home. I could almost feel and see the change in this crowd, Their voices seemed solemn yet happy when they spoke. As they walked back home, each step seemed filled with the lightness of a child confident the world around was what it should be.

Mama explained to me that this tradition of blessing food began with royalty, when they had to make sure their food was not poisoned. Whether this is true or not, I never questioned. Our food was never blessed before Halina and I made that trek to the church, and we never became ill. Perhaps Mama and Tata's faith in God had a lot to do with that bit of luck. I do know for certain that after Babsha died, Mama became a bit more faithful to attending mass on Sunday. Our Easter food was also blessed every Holy Saturday for those next five years after Babsha's death.

That summer seemed more glorious then ever. Babsha and I spent more time together. Mama even found time to join us on walks through Sherman Park. On our week-end travels to sit on those grassy knolls near Lake Michigan, Babsha, who before had little desire to join us, did so now. Although she preferred sitting on a bench, she did seem to find great pleasure in dipping her bare feet in the cool water, laughing heartily each time a small wave lapped against her bare legs.

Many times now, I think how nice it would have been if we had been aware that this would be her last summer with us. Our trips, our talks, our quiet evenings outdoors certainly may have lasted longer. We enjoyed each other so much—I cannot remember any vulgar words ever spoken in our home—no heavy arguments between adults. So perhaps I should be grateful that indeed we were living life to the fullest—as though this, our last summer together.

Babsha left Chicago during the third week of September. Her good-byes to friends on our block were tender with wishes of a safe trip and tears of hating to see her go. I remember clearly how she held Halina on her lap that last day, hugging her close, as though hating to release the pleasure of holding this small child. Finally, kissing Halina's cheek and telling her how much she was loved, Babsha stood and walked to where I sat on the kitchen radiator watching her departing embraces. She knelt down in front of me and said: 'Ya cie bardzo kocham,moia mala.' I jumped down from the radiator and wrapped my arms around her neck when she said those words—'I love you very much my dearest little one.' She held me close and kissed me good-bye. Mama, standing by the kitchen door, Babsha's suitcase sitting on the floor next to her, said in Polish: 'Before you know it, Babsha will return. By the end of October we will have her back again.'

'Tak, tak.' Babsha nodded, saying yes, yes in Polish. We had gone through this the Sunday before with Aunt Isabelle and her family. Our Sunday dinner on that day was filled with best wishes for a happy journey. This last week seemed to fly by. Here it was, another Sunday and more final good-byes. Tata was downstairs in the garage, sitting in his car, waiting for Babsha. Mama, Halina and I would not be going to the train station, Babsha said it would be too hectic. There were no tears with this departure. Mama and Tata were looking forward to a great celebration when Babsha returned at the end of October.

Because Babsha spoke almost no English at all, she carried a letter of introduction, written by my cousin, Alfreda. Babsha could present that letter to almost anyone in New York. The letter asked she be directed to the port where a liner sat waiting to take passengers to a port of entry near Poland. Of course, once she arrived in Poland, her communication problems would end. Babsha had cousins and in-laws still living there. Upon her arrival in Czestohowa a cousin would meet her.

What were the feelings Babsha had, or the thoughts, as she stood on the deck of that liner and looked out over that same ocean she crossed once so many years ago. A journey that not only brought her to a strange land but also took her away from the man and country she loved. I know her conviction that she gave her daughters, and any future generation after, the freedom she sought on that journey never faltered. Yet sadness must have been her companion on the voyage back. In giving she also gave up so much. The journey back so different…a warm cabin, the joy of stepping on deck at any time to look at the vast blue water as it blended with a far off horizon. The glory in each sunset and sunrise. Having this now, she surely must have relived the pain of that journey spent in steerage.

Once Babsha reached the country of her birth and childhood, the delightful joy she felt no doubt mingled with the sorrow that consumed her as she knelt beside her husband's grave. So all of this, the journey, the recollections, the grief, and yes, even the abundance of joy, all of it and any of it may have led to making this her final journey here on earth as well.

That Halloween I was allowed to go trick or treating during early evening hours. Before this, Mama only allowed day time carousing on this day. Tata evidently considered me old enough and had no qualms that our neighborhood was a safe place for early evening door to door trick or treating. I took one of Mama's old dresses, cinched a belt tightly around my waist, pulled the dress over it until it no longer dragged along the floor, and my costume was almost complete. One of Babsha's wool shawls and her old purse completed my outfit. When I opened the purse, two nickels shone up at me. I knew Babsha had left them in there especially for me, as she had before when I played 'dress-up'. During one of our final walks, I told her what I planned on wearing for Halloween. She suggested I use this very purse. Now I could treat Rosemary to some penny candy. Before going out this evening, Tata, Halina and I had a bowl of chicken soup and homemade noodles. Tata was unusually quiet. Some terrible news took Mama away on a trip to New York City. In my child's mind, I knew something was wrong, but could not comprehend the sadness until days later—and months after. On this evening I was more anxious to get out for an evening of fun then wonder 'what' was happening.

There were never too many trick or treats in this ethnic neighborhood. We picked up the traditions of Halloween through heresay. Children always carried a bar of soap for smearing up store windows; some even carried eggs to throw at doors. As always, the wrong message was sent to those who knew little the real meaning of Halloween. Mama, as most in our neighborhood, would not hear of such terrible tricks to play on someone, in fact, except for one or two ruffians, as Mama called them, most children displayed courteous behavior and showed respect for neighbors property. 'You will not resort to being a ruffian like the boys next door.' Mama always seemed to equate vandalism with the boys next door, ever since the robbery we had in our home just that past summer. I myself preferred stopping at Slatky's and purchasing candy then roaming through the neighborhood with Rosemary just looking at the costumes other children wore. I knew for my two nickels, Miss Slatky would put enough candy in the little brown bag worth much more. If Rosemary and I did witness any neighbors passing out oranges or apples, we would naturally stop by that home as well.

This year Mama would not be at home to hear of my glorious Halloween evening. Two days earlier she received a telegram from the port authorities on Ellis Island. Babsha had had a heart attack aboard the liner bringing her home. Rushed to a hospital in New York City, Mama and Aunt Isabelle were advised to come as soon as possible to that hospital. Babsha 's prognosis was not good. Mama and Aunt Isabelle departed for New York City the very next day.

Mama would always refer to this trip, which included her very first ride on a subway, 'a trip through hell'.

Babsha suffered another heart attack after Mama and Aunt Isabelle arrived. A third heart attack took Babsha's life on All Saints Day. I thought the day of her death very appropriate. This was a woman who never asked for more then a better life for her two daughters. She never complained…about anything. Her gratitude was as bright and warm as sunlight; her love and joy as constant as a sunset and sunrise. As she lay in her coffin, wearing that familiar dark dress with its little white collar, I kissed her forehead and bid her a sad good-bye…and finally realized.

At first glance she looked so peacefully sound asleep. I hardly imagined this face would never light up and smile at me again. Only when I touched her icy hand, the fingers now forever cold in stillness, I knew her warm hand of love would never hold mine again. Our walks through the park, forever gone. When I kissed her good-bye and my lips felt the stone cold forehead, I knew the feel of her warm lips would never again press against my forehead in a good-morning or good-night kiss. Later, at the cemetery, as the closed casket was lowered into the ground, I knew that part of my glorious innocent childhood without worries or cares, went into the ground with her that cold November day. My sweet Babsha was gone. She was only fifty-six years old.

There are those who believe a full and hearty wake gives testament to how much the deceased was loved and/or respected during life. On the day of Babsha's funeral, our flat was filled with people. Those bearing food and those giving their final respects. Everyone on our block knew of Babsha's death; and since Tata's morning route had been suspended the day Mama went to New York, the bakery now closed for days because of Babsha's death, many others in the neighborhood arrived on this day. They all paid honor to this sweet loving person who graced our neighborhood with her quiet unobtrusive charm.

1934 THROUGH 1938

Conversations between Tata and Mama were often beyond my comprehension: Once they spoke of a bank robber named Dillinger. Tata read in his Polish paper that this man had been shot and killed as he left a Chicago movie theater. Another time, when we attended our city's Century of Progress Exposition and Tata commented profusely on Sally Rand and her fan dance. Mama waved off his comments with 'oh stop already. It is not as though you have never seen a stripper before this.' Apparently Tata often frequented the strip shows downtown during his bachelor days, so Mama told me years later.

But the world of gangsters, strippers, racial tension and cultural differences were so out of the realm of my world at this time, I listened to these conversations with only half an ear. When my parents spoke of their disenchantment with the Polish Choir, I was more inclined to understanding their sudden detachment from what was a regular gathering place for friends. The old crowd was quickly vanishing, some completely gone as people moved to other areas of Chicago. Fresh young faces were arriving with fresh ideas on what they wanted from these gatherings. Mama and Tata's dear friend, Mr. Gongolova passed away from a sudden heart attack and Mr. Chmielewski seemed to complain a great deal about the pain in his back. As their world was changing, so was mine. I tried always to listen to Mama's words when she emphasized how we must accept change and hope for the best.

Loomis Street was paved now. Only the cobbled side streets remained. Within a short time those street would be paved as well. Still feeling the sadness of Babsha's death, Mama and Tata decided to spend New Years Eve of '33 at home. We all went out to any early supper at one of Tata's favorite Polish restaurants on Milwaukee Avenue, then later attended a movie in the Loop. By ten that evening we were back home and settled in its warmth. Our Christmas tree was still up; it always came down after the holiday of the Three Kings in January. Although we all felt that slight melancholia of not having Babsha with us, Mama reminded us she would not have wanted us to be so despondent. 'She will stay in our hearts forever. But as she often said, life must go on despite those sad circumstances we have little control over.' So as I snuggled close to Mama on this New Years Eve, I felt grateful to have my parents home this year to celebrate the coming of 1934. Mama told us of her plans to convert the back bedroom into a sitting room. Sometime in the new year coming, Halina and I would be sharing the middle bedroom. Since I was the oldest, the privilege of sleeping on the right side of the bed, that side close to the window, would go to me. By the end of January, the change took place.

On cold winter mornings, when crackling frost covered our bedroom window, I always felt such a great sense of security snuggling beneath that familiar quilt and listening to St. Augustine's bell toll six A.M. Pulling the quilt closer to my face, I inhaled the familiar scent that still permeated the material. That mild smell of lemon glycerine soap that Babsha used still lingered on this quilt. I would close my eyes and smile as in my mind I said good-morning to her.

Janauary of 1934 was a month of many changes. Added to the newly repainted porch and hallway Tata now planned to cover the floor and steps with linoleum. Spring would bring a repainting of woodwork throughout the entire flat; new carpeting added to the dining and living room areas, and an electric box to keep our food cold would replace the faithful green ice-box.

To make room for our new electric box, the little black stove had to be removed from its spot in our kitchen and sold to a junk dealer. I felt rather sorry seeing it carried away. To never again watch those dancing flames behind the little windows…to never feel its warmth when I came in from the winter cold, it felt as though a close friend was leaving our flat. Mama felt none of this. 'The soot from that stove was a constant problem to my clean kitchen floor. How nice to finally not have worries about laying newspapers on my freshly scrubbed floor during cold weather days when everyone tramped into the kitchen without removing their boots, just to warm themselves by this stove.' That dream of not putting newspapers down did not end as fast as she hoped. Mama continued doing just that when it rained outdoors as well.

Of course, it took only a short time for our new electric box to take claim to the little stoves place of honor. And I too realized the exchange was well worth the loss. Our food stayed colder and fresher and Mama did not have to shop two to three times a week. How grand to reach in and pour myself a glass of milk that now stayed as cold in summer as it had in winter, when we usually placed the bottle of milk outside the little kitchen window. Something Mama hated doing now since our 'falling out', so to speak, with the Koczubowski family next door.

It happened the summer before, on the kind of a warm Saturday evening that drove families to sitting outdoors. Humidity hung in the air as though heaven had strung a line of wash across the city. Mama, Tata and Babsha were sitting in their respective kitchen chairs, Halina and I on the front stoop of the bakery front. We were all hoping for a sudden change in the air. Perhaps a breeze off Lake Michigan or a shift from the now southern stir to a greater northern one. Next door, in Koczubowski's Tavern the music was loud and constant. A wedding reception was taking place and with the warm air, all doors and windows were wide open. Despite the fact that it was Saturday, and we had already enjoyed a bowl of ice-cream which Mama purchased from the grocery store across the street, the hour was getting late. My eyes felt heavy, and Halina was fussing.

Mama finally stood and said she was going upstairs to open all the windows. 'Perhaps by the time we get to sleep it will be a bit cooler.'

What took place next should have been a clear indication to all of us on how the world around was changing. Especially our serene neighborhood. Mama was gone for what seemed only a few minutes. When she came bounding out of the gangway and in a somber yet fright filled voice said to Tata: 'Someone broke into our kitchen window. I was sure it was locked before we came outdoors…both sides are flung open now…'Tata stood up immediately and without a word rushed back through the gangway and upstairs. The rest of us followed; Babsha holding

Halina by the hand, Mama and I closely behind as I grasped her hand tightly. The sight Tata discovered when he reached our upstairs flat was not a pleasant one.

The large trunk in Tata and Mama's bedroom had been broken open. All the coral jewelry his mother gave him when Tata left Poland—gone; silver dollars he had been saving—gone; dresser scarves and handkerchiefs with colorful tatted edges, worked on by my great-grandmother and Babsha, all gone.' Who did this Mama?' was all I could ask. Mama shrugged, tears running down her cheeks as Babsha put an arm around her shoulder, trying to console her. Tata's face was red with anger when he stepped back into the kitchen and went to the little window above the radiator. 'The Koczubowski boys. They are the only ones who know where this window leads. Who else?' Tata concluded.. Mama shook her head. 'But how can you be so sure?'

'I cannot. But I will go and ask Mr. and Mrs. Koczubowski to address their sons on this matter. For if not their boys, then surely the boys they hang out with. The entire neighborhood knows how wild they have become since reaching their teen years. Their drunken behavior since age fourteen may have now turned to this—thievery. I will talk to them. Now. '

Perhaps Tata hoped that as parents, Mr. and Mrs. Koczubowski would know the whereabouts of their children that evening. Or, at least, have enough authority that the boys would tell the truth. Tata was that sure of who committed this crime. When he returned, exactly a half hour later, he knew the stolen goods would never be returned, or even found…let alone an accounting on who committed the robbery.

'They were angry that I even suggested their sons had done this. They took me through every room in that place and I saw nothing to prove my suspicions. The boys were at the bar drinking. When they saw me they only nodded and smiled. I could see clearly by the look they gave that they knew why I was there. But what proof did I have? None.'

'Shall we go to the police with this?' Mama asked him, crying again at the loss. She knew nothing could ever be replaced. All those precious items has been tucked away for safe keeping until the day Halina and I were married.

'It would be useless.' Tata answered. 'All we can hope for now is that the parents of these boys will soon find out what they are. Perhaps one day our valuables will be returned.'

Of course, that day never came. After this incident and his confrontation with Mr. Koczubowski, Tata never again spoke to anyone in that family. As to myself, this was my first insight into what I might expect in that world outside my safe haven. So this, the sad reason why Mama was happy not to rely on using the roof next door to keep food cold.

Of course, we soon realized how much heat the little stove provided to our kitchen. Now Tata had to remove the door between the kitchen and the dining area. We dare not close off that large kitchen from the back of the flat. With only one long radiator in the living room, and one below the window in the kitchen, heat had to go in an unencumbered flow from front to back.

That January my life of a leisure childhood also came to an end. For the past few months Mama began adding chores to my growing years. Carrying ashes from our furnace became one of the newest.

Tata kept four bushel baskets in the basement below the downstairs kitchen. He used the baskets for those ashes he shoveled out of the large furnace that heated our home.

Tata and Mama always carried out this chore alone. Tata would fill the bushel basket half way, for filled it would be much too heavy. Then he and Mama carried the basket up the steps, out the kitchen door, through the gangway and garage, out to the garbage can in the alley. When I became old enough to help with this chore, I took Tata's place in helping Mama with the basket. Of course, when I helped, Tata never filled the basket as much as when he and Mama carried it.

Because of its narrowness, carrying that bushel through the gangway was tricky. Mama had to walk ahead, I following behind, the basket between us. We stumbled along rather clumsily, but finally reached the garage door. Opening this large wood door was less hectic then walking through our gangway with the ashes. The entire door opened in the center and folded unto itself like an accordion. This was very convenient on a very cold windy day when I also had the chore of throwing out daily garbage. All we had to do was open enough of that door so that we could step out into the alley. Dumping our furnace ashes into the garbage can was quite another matter.

The can, for one thing, was taller then me. I could usually reach up and toss a brown bag of garbage over the edge, but helping Mama lift this bushel filled with ashes…well, that took a bit of analyzing. First Mama had to determine which way the wind was blowing, making sure we lifted the bushel with the wind at our back. I tried to lift it as high as possible, with Mama finally completing the dumping by herself. Despite all her precautions, some ashes never failed to come back at us. The trips to that garbage can seemed endless, and by the time we finished, I felt as sooty as the inside of our furnace. I could only think how lucky my sister was that she got to stay in the nice warm basement with Tata while Mama and I trudged to the alley. Soon this chore would have to be reserved for Saturdays. This January my week days would be occupied in a large red building on 47th. and Paulina.

Mama and I often talked about the day when I would begin school. She took to sitting in that little nook that Babsha once occupied. I of course still clung to that cubby hole at the other end of this showcase window. Whenever we were alone, Mama and I conversed in English, which made me forever grateful to her. I would be six years old in February, and although I spoke the English language, my reading and writing capabilities were very limited. Mama, at best, taught me the alphabet, so it was only those letters I practiced diligently before starting first grade.

Hamline School was no stranger to me. Every time we went shopping on Ashland Avenue, Mama made a point of passing this building and pointing it out to me. By the time I was ready to begin first grade in January, the route we took would be a very familiar one for me: across 49th Place, past the coal yard on my right, an empty warehouse on my left. Then under the viaduct and across 48th Place. Straight down 48th and Loomis to 47th Place, where I turned left, and on to Paulina Street. There it stood, a red two story brick with a deep basement and a high iron fence surrounding it completely. A structure whose contents would shape much of my life, change many of my beliefs and introduce me to a country and world I never knew about or even imagined.

My walk to school took me through a neighborhood much the same as the block I lived on. For those first five years of my life, I only knew those people who lived on my street, a few around the block, and those who were friends of Mama's and Tata's. On this January day in 1934 I was about to meet children who came from a variety of cultures. Some of what I knew of on Loomis, others quite different from what had settled on our block.

Although most Polish families in our neighborhood sent their children to St. John of God parochial school, there were those, such as Mama and Tata, who preferred a public school education for their children. In a few years that would also change, when St. Augustine would introduce first through eight grade for children of German heritage. For now, families from this Back of the Yards district melting pot settled for public school.

To begin first grade in any public school at this time, a child had to be either six years of age, or their birthday close to that age on the day school began. There were two starting semesters: one in January, another in August. Since my birthday fell in February, I fell into the semester starting in January. Thankfully, Rosemary, who's birthday was in January, also fell into that same category. Quite obviously many other children as well, from the size of our class on that first day.

Mama walked me to school that day, but not directly to the classroom. Mama knew ahead of time which door was meant for first through fourth graders. This was where she left me, standing in line with all the other children, waiting to begin their first day at Hamline.

As most of the children who began school this day, I was freshly bathe, combed, my cotton dress starched and pressed. I knew how to dress and undress in my winter outfit of snowsuit, boots, mittens, cap and scarf, so I had no fear of wondering who

I would ask to help me. An older student, standing just inside the large double door, came out shortly before the school bell rang, and guided this little group of first graders up the steps and to the first grade classroom. We were immediately told to enter the cloak room just behind our classroom, remove our winter garb, hang it up on hooks and then proceed to a desk in the classroom.

With prosperity still a great distance off for many families, I now came face to face with that small percentage of children who came from extreme poverty. Also those from families where the bread winner found more solace on Saloon Alley then in his home. These were the children without boots, with tattered clothing, some unkempt, and hardly ready to begin their first day at school.

Hamline School was well equipped to help such children. Especially built for families without bathing facilities, showers were located in the basement of this school. Much the same as the ones at Sherman Park, there for families who had no other place to bathe. A school nurse gathered the neglected children, separating boys and girls, and took each group to shower in the basement. Within an hour they returned with faces fresh and clean, hair combed, quite often with a new outfit of clothing, and hopefully a better outlook on the beginning day. Breakfast was given freely by the public school system at this time, regardless of family income. Each morning, every child grades one through four, received a small bottle of milk plus two or three crackers. For those who had to eat lunch in school, the cost was three cents when I started school...up to five cents by the time I graduated. It was always free to those who could not afford to pay.

Indoor bathroom facilities were still absent from some homes on my block. Just as those who had to use showers in school, I could not help but know who used showers provided by the park district. Twice a week Emily and her family, Elaine and her mother, the elderly couple across the street...all went with towel in hand, a bar of soap in the other, on their way to Sherman Park. Most of the time, usually during the summer months, it was early in the morning. When autumn and winter came, their trek to the showers changed to afternoon hours. I always felt a great sense of gratitude that I did not have to bathe in a public facility.

My first day at school was exciting. I could hardly wait until I returned home to tell Mama about the new friends I met. Angelina, a little Italian girl with braided hair that looked as blue-black as the coal Tata shoveled into our furnace, sat in the desk directly in front of mine. Katherine, blue-eyed with fiery red hair, sat in back of me. The first time I raised my hand to be excused because I had to use the bathroom, teacher picked Angelina to accompany me. We were never allowed to leave the room alone.

I adored listening to Angelina speak, her accent was so unusual. Of course, I never realized I spoke with a strange accent as well. When Angelina went home that day she no doubt told her mother and father about the little Polish girl with a strange accent she had befriended that day. Angelina came from a poor family. The flimsy coat she wore in winter looked more suitable for a spring day. Thankfully, beneath the coat she wore a thick sweater of red wool, knitted by her mother. When I introduced her to Rosemary during that first recess, we all got on splendidly. Rosemary promised to bring her jump rope to school the following day so we could enjoy our half hour recess more fully.

Katherine was not as easy to talk to. She rather kept to herself that first week of school. Rosemary talked about her quiet behavior quite often as we walked home from school. One day we decided to merely approach her and ask her if she would like to play with us. Surprisingly, we found her as open and outgoing as Angelina. When my first week in school ended, I mentioned all of this to Mama. 'Many times that is the best way to make new friends, especially with people who seem shy.' I knew what she meant, for I was just as shy, most of the time. Rosemary was the one who really approached Katherine on that day, but it was with me that Katherine barred her soul.

The stories we exchanged about our home life helped me better understand what Mama often said: 'New friends that are different is like walking into a garden of many flowers. Learn to enjoy all of them. Like the colors of a rainbow, they will brighten your life.' And she was right. Even Jose, a little

Mexican boy who spoke no English at all and was darker then any other child in our classroom, brightened our room of pale faces. Jose loved to contort his features into funny faces…those that made us laugh. He would run up to all of the girls during recess time, make his funny face, then quickly run away. By the end of that first half semester, Jose learned enough English to inform us he was playing matador. The little girls he teased with his funny faces, he explained, were the pretty little bulls he hoped would chase him. Full and chubby on the day he started school, Jose grew into quite a handsome looking young man by the time we graduated from grammar school. I often wondered what sort of home life Jose had, and often wished he had told me about it, just as Katherine did, when we also walked to the restroom together.

Katherine, in my eyes, was not as fortunate as Angelina, who although very poor, came from a loving family. Although her clothes were thin and flimsy for winter wear, they were always clean and ironed. Her black hair was neatly braided and her pale olive skin so shiny from being freshly scrubbed. When she talked of the marvelous meals her mother and aunt cooked and the wine she was allowed to have at each evening meal, my hunger came long before lunch time. Anglina seemed gloriously happy and had a special gift of brightening the day, no matter how gloomy the weather outdoors.

Katherine, who was by far the brightest student in our class of twenty children, was also one of the children the nurse took to shower each morning. Her fabulous red hair never looked combed, and her hands and faced at times looked as though they had gone unwashed for days. The first time she told me about her family I could only listen wide-eyed with wondering if the story were true.

Her father, who worked for one of the large meat packing companies, came home drunk almost every night. Beside Katherine, there were two younger children at home. Her mother, from what Katherine said, tried so hard to keep some order in their three room flat. 'Which is hard to do, since me mother enjoys drinking as well.' Katherine always added wistfully. I wondered who cared for her and the other children, but dare not pry. Instead I broached Mama with the question. 'Someone up above is watching over this family. She no doubt needed a friend like you to talk with. Keep listening, that is all you can do. Perhaps one day her life will grow better.'

I never knew if or when that happened. By sixth grade I met Angelina's out-going boisterous family. Their home reminded me of my own…well kept and smelling delicious of cleanliness and cooking. I never got to meet Katherine's family. One day she seemed to blossom into a beautiful young lady and gave herself the care her mother neglected to do. The death of her father came after a night of heavy drinking. From what I heard, he stepped in front of a trolley car and was killed instantly. When Katherine's mother died a year later of a heart attack, Katherine and her siblings were sent to live with an aunt in Wisconsin. Perhaps now, I could only hope, Katherine's life improved.

During that first semester, Angelina, Rosemary and I were close friends. Like myself, Angelina was born in Chicago. She lived closer to Ashland Avenue in a home her father bought shortly after migrating to America from Italy. Angelina was the oldest of four children. They lived in a two story home where both flats had to share one bathroom, which was located in a downstairs hall. Her mother did all their laundry by hand on a scrub board. Mama also did this with heavily soiled laundry, so this was not strange news to me. Angelina's joy came one day when she told me excitedly about the new electric iron her uncle purchased for the women of the house. I felt her joy when she told me about this. I knew how much ironing Mama always had and could not imagine life without this appliance.

When we all got to know each other in this classroom of different cultural backgrounds and classes began, our differences ended. We were all here to learn the same thing: how to speak, read and write the English language; to learn about our country and to appreciate each others differences. If anyone was created to give us a marvelous beginning to this new education, it was Mrs. Walsh.

Mrs. Walsh made sure on that very first day of school we all understood why we were here and what was expected of us. For those who spoke little or no English, (Jose actually being the only one who did not), Mrs.Walsh sent a note home to the parents with the same message she gave us that day, in hopes someone might translate her words: 'just as my parents and grandparents, yours also sacrificed a great deal to make sure you lived in a country filled with an abundance of freedom and choices. Now you have a chance to use this freedom and make a choice: listen and learn and become good citizens of this country, or, stay asleep and learn nothing. The sacrifice your parents made will be lost if you choose to stay lazy and sleep. For most of you learning will come easily. I will always be here to help those who find learning a bit more difficult. All of you must depend on help from your parents or friends in your community. Whatever you do, the choice is yours. I am here to teach and help all of you.' Her message of course was loud and clear: if we did not pay attention, we would not only be a disappointment to our parents, but worst yet, to ourselves as well.

The public school system at this time did not cater to other languages. We attended school as one…all of us Americans. For those who wished to continue educating children in their roots ethnic language, the settlement house or family provided this education. Public schools took care of our English education, and provided other care as well.

Not only that shower in the basement for those neglected children, but visiting nurses and dentists as well. Both came to the school on the average of once a week. The nurse provided children with free medical care, the dentist with free dental care. I remember the day Halina started first grade and came home with lice in her hair. It did not take long for Mama to get to the corner drug store on 48th and Loomis to purchase a special liquid for lice removal. The brown wash smelled terrible. I felt sure it was this alone that killed the lice. After that, at least once a month, Mama checked our hair to make sure we were free of the nasty critters. Of course, by then the visiting nurse had things under control. Notes and special fine combs for lice removal went home with each child, plus full instructions on proper care of a childs hair. Later, when proper indoor plumbing and bathing facilities were installed in every home, the problem of lice began to quickly fade.

Free dental care continued until I reached fourth grade. It was available to every student. This too declined when jobs became more available and people were working again. Then too, many families preferred a family dentist rather then the one offered through the school.

Low cost and free lunches stayed around for quite awhile. Mama always preferred Halina and I go home for lunch. But there were days, especially in severe winter weather, that she allowed us to stay in school for lunch. I felt thrilled on those days. Everything was so different and new to me. Sitting at the long wooden table, which was a large replica of what is known as a picnic bench today, I ate hot dogs and beans, or spaghetti and meat balls, in happy wonder. This was a type of food we never had at home.

Children, especially the lower grades, were always well behaved. The knicker clad boys who yelled and ran around non-stop at recess time, dare not misbehave during class hours or lunch time. While the yelling and running about, and knocking each other to the ground, startled me at first, I accepted it as a 'boy thing' as time went on. For after all, I had never before been witness to such a display of high energy and noise. Always in the company of adults, the children I knew behaved. The friends I had on my block, except for Wishniewski's and Koczubowski's wild brood, whom I never considered close friends, such rough play never showed itself in my company.

When that school bell rang...in the morning, during recess, or at the end of the day, all grew quiet. Girls to the cloak room first, boys next. Once dressed, girls lined up single file on one side of the room, boys on the other. Quietly, no talking whatsoever, we marched in and out of that building several times a day, with upper-class students acting as monitors. They of course relished the power of authority to write down the name of any child who stepped out of line or talked out of turn. Of course, any time we could sneak in a whisper or two, or extend an arm or leg out and get away with it...we felt gleefully wicked.

Those eight years in Hamline were joyous for me. Mrs. Doyle's first grade class began the love affair I found with learning. Perhaps because she was about the same age as Mama, I felt a sense of security in following her instructions so closely. I also thought her remarkably clever. Not only knowledgeable in what we needed to purchase in order to continue this new education, she also learned all of our names in one day…and changed mine as well.

Each child stood and gave their full name that first day of school. For those few children who pronounced their name in full ethnicity, Mrs. Walsh found little trouble translating to an English pronunciation. When my turn came to say 'Prczeslawa Leonia Kalinowski', Mrs. Walsh put a finger to her pursed lips and said ' well, now…' as questioning as the frown on her forehead. 'I will send a note home to your mother requesting you bring in your birth certificate. I have a dear friend who is quite adept in translating foreign names to an English version.' I simply nodded and sat down. For Mama had warned me days before that this might happen.

'Just as my name was changed on the day we arrived at Ellis Island, I had no doubt yours would be changed as well. Tata insisted on this given name. Who was I to argue?' So the next day I presented my birth certificate to Mrs. Walsh. By the third day of that first week in school, I had my new name.

'The closest my friend came to what your name is in English is Priscilla Leona. I will write a note to you mother and see if this change is agreeable with her.' Which it was. And so from that day my legal name became: Priscilla Leona Kalinowski. To Mama and Tata, my relatives and their friends, I remained 'Lonia' for a long time after. Although I thought Priscilla a very romantic sounding name, my friends immediately dubbed me with the nickname of 'Pris.' A nickname I detested but learned to live with. The day would come when that too would be changed, to Pat. But that is another story. For now, through grammar school and high school, I walked around with two names: my middle name and my new legal name.

New friends during those three years at Hamline never became as close to me as Rosemary. For one thing Mama never allowed me to stray too far from our block at such an early age. After school, on week-ends and during summer vacation, Rosemary was the only friend I had to roller skate with, jump rope or play hop-scotch with, or visit, either at her home or mine. Eddie and Clement often joined in our conversations, but they considered most of what we did strictly 'girl-stuff'. Not until I reached fourth grade and age nine did my adventures broaden to other blocks and new adventures.

For someone like me, who never had an English book to read, and the English alphabet as the only written word, so to speak, all the newness of my English education fascinated me. All this new reading and writing was about to become a new friend as well. One that would keep me company for the rest of my life during quiet times and lonely times. That simple task of learning to write my new name was miraculous in itself; the joy of learning to read English opened up a new world to me.

When I purchased my first pen point and little wooden holder, a bottle of ink, pencil and eraser, and began writing in that special tablet provided by the school, I felt electrified that the words kept in my mind and spoken in English were now transferred to this piece of paper. I had written the Polish alphabet many times, and Mama was diligent in teaching me the English alphabet. Now, as I began to read 'See Jane run. See Jack Run. See baby play, then writing every word down in that perfect penmanship demanded by Mrs. Walsh, I soon became obsessed and devoted to writing and spelling every new word I learned, correctly. Industrious even on week-ends, I sat in my little cubby hole practicing the circles and slashes, all perfectly centered between two lines, so that all those new words looked as splendid as they sounded. My education, many times, took precedence over paper dolls and coloring books.

But not all was as sweet as reading and writing. At best, I tolerated geography. All those other countries seemed so far away. I was hardly interested in what grew there or what industry dominated each nation. History was a subject far more tolerable and enjoyable, especially the stories of how the United States came to be. Until now my history lessons were always about Poland. Now I could go home and tell Mama and Tata of a country they knew so little about.

The fundamentals of math...addition, subtraction, multiplication, division, all were pounded into our heads from day one. "You must at least know the basics.' Mrs. Walsh insisted. 'No matter what you decide to do with your life, those basics of math are important.' Later, at about sixth grade, boys were more encouraged then girls to continue on with higher math. Most girls were expected to either get married or do no more then clerical work or clerk in a department store. For a few lucky ones, such as Mrs. Walsh, they went on to become teachers, or nurses. For those not as lucky, extended math was a frivolous endeavor. This unfortunate conclusion no doubt hurt many young girls, their thinking no doubt warped against math just as mine was: the basics were good enough...I never tried any harder then that.

Each day, when I returned home from school, or came home for lunch, I was full of exciting things to talk about: my new friends, their family life, and all the wonderful new subjects I was learning.

By the time Halina was old enough to join me in going to school each morning, Tata and Mama broke away from the Polish Choir completely. Although they still continued to see many of their friends, the get-togethers were either at our home, a friends home, or an occasional supper at a Polish restaurant. Food, as always, was not only the center of such gatherings, it remained a worthy subject in family life. It was about this time that one of Tata's favorite dishes became rabbit meat.

Seeing a skinned and frozen rabbit carcass hanging from a hook in front of a butcher shop as we strolled along Ashland Avenue during the winter was one thing. After all, this was a place to purchase any form of raw meat from almost any form of animal. Tata's remarkable appetite brought on a new hobby. One that would put a new light on rabbit meat.

Tata may have preferred raising pigeons in the attic, for once or twice he mentioned this to Mama. Of course, she would never relent to that awful smell again. So one day he settled on three rabbits, two female, one male. The hut he built for them sat in the basement below the downstairs kitchen. Every evening after supper, which we usually ate in that little kitchen during the week, Tata would go down into the basement and feed his rabbits with lettuce and any other food he thought might please and fatten them. In my childs mind, I looked upon the rabbits as a pet akin to our dog Berek, or the cats we kept around the house...or the canaries Mama tried to raise, without much luck. Berek died from old age and the cats we housed gave us precious moments with litters of adorable kittens...which Tata gave away. There was no neutering a this time, and Tata looked upon the cats as only there for hunting mice...and, unfortunately, Mama's canaries. No matter where she placed that canary cage, our clever hunters somehow managed to capture those poor little birds. Mama eventually grew tired of picking up yellow feathers while our cat sat in the corner licking her paws. And now we had Tata's rabbits.

I rather looked forward to going into the basement with Tata and feeding the soft, cuddly looking creatures. It was one Sunday evening, after spending a week-end sleep-over at Rosemary's house, that Tata'a hobby vanished. The bunnies and their cage were no longer in the basement. Mama's only explanation at the time, that Tata found they were too much trouble. Much later, about my second year in high school, Mama finally confessed to the real reason the rabbits vanished so quickly.

The Friday that I left to spent a week-end sleep at Rosemary's house, Tata decided it was time for a rabbit meat meal. The chosen victim, one of the female rabbits. Mama never went into detail on how Tata went about killing that rabbit, but apparently she helped him. 'When he slit the rabbit's belly open and I saw the little babies just developing, I put a hand to my mouth to hold back a scream. Thank God Halina stayed upstairs in the kitchen, playing with her toys. I turned to your Tata and tried to stay as calm as possible when I said: "Leon, look at this...how could you be so cruel?" Of course, he had no idea the rabbit was pregnant. But that was it. I told him I did not want any of this meat on my table and to get rid of the rabbits immediately.'

When I heard this story, I felt thankful I had not been there, or that it was never talked about again. Come to think of it, I do not remember Tata ever eating rabbit meat after that day.

When it came to family matters, Tata's sights stayed on a more pleasant and straighter course. He encouraged whatever Mama deemed necessary in furthering her daughters cultural or artistic talents, such as they were, from music to singing. When I reached my sixth birthday, Mama decided since I showed so much enthusiasm in dancing when attending Polish classes at the settlement, perhaps I might show some talent in tap dancing. But dancing the Krakowiak in a circle with childish abandonment is a far cry from tap shoes and intricate tapping steps. How I managed to get through even one month and one recital of tapping display still puzzles me today. When I stood on that stage with a group of about ten other wanna-be-Elinor Powells and tapped to the tune of 'Hey Young Fella, You Better Get Your Old Umbrella', I felt rather proud. The day after our recital, when our instructor decided it was time to introduce some acrobatic skills into our tapping repertoire, my career ended. Never very athletic, I begged Mama to relieve me of the possibility of hurting my body, or shaming myself in any one of the tumbling lessons soon to follow. Surely I was meant for some other form of artistic ability besides doing splits and bending backwards, I pleaded. Mama relented. Happily, I continued with what I felt a safer choice...roller skating, jumping rope and continued fascination with reading and writing.

Sunday funnies became an important part of my reading program. Little Orphan Annie, Dick Tracy. and of course the first Superman Comic that came out in 1938. These plus many more added to my list of reading pleasure. Later, as I matured and discovered the public library at Sherman Park, I concentrated more on checking out books with more regularity then reading comics.

My chores around the house increased as years were added to my life. Helping Mama hang the wash in our back attic; scrubbing the kitchen floor every Friday during summer vacation, and the most enjoyable chore, watering Tata's tree and the small plot of grass that grew in front of our bakery. Whenever Mama finished sweeping the walk and gutter every morning, I found hosing down the sidewalk a most relaxing chore.

On cooler days I still wore my overalls with a blouse beneath. When watering the sidewalk, I always took off my shoes and socks. To stand there, hose in hand, the water swishing away all the dust, what could possibly feel better then the hot sidewalk beneath my bare feet turning deliciously cool as it grew wet with every drop of sparkling water. The sweet smell of that green grass as it grew wet, the musty smell of the wet bark on Tata's tree. If I closed my eyes and ran my fingers beneath that water coming from the hose, I could dream I was standing in my own forest of green grass, tall trees and a water fall, and I the only one to care for them. What a peaceful and splendid way to begin a summer day.

One thing I never did was help Mama cook. That was a skill I had to learn on my own after marriage. Yet perhaps I learned more from just watching then I realized. From the very first meal I cooked and cake I baked, the gift of both continues to be something I still enjoy immensely.

More and more I became aware of how Mama took care of Tata. She prepared the food he liked best, cared for our home with exceptional cleanliness and love, and spent time with her family in love and devotion. From the earliest years of my life I was convinced this was all it took to make a perfect family, or for me to be that perfect wife. Of course, much later in life, I found it took more then that. That again, is quite another story.

Just before the Christmas of my seventh birthday, Tata hired a man to help with repairs around our house. His name was Felix, and he was a master carpenter. He not only helped Tata, Felix also built a Christmas gift for Halina and me. A charming little table, two chairs and a small matching hutch. All the pieces were painted pale aqua. All had intricate designs of little leaves and flowers carved on the chair backs, table trim, and hutch drawers. This would be our Christmas gift for this Eve. To this set Santa added a lovely little ceramic tea set. Halina, Rosemary and I always invited Eddie and Clement over for afternoon tea, which Mama kindly brewed for us, plus a few of her fresh baked cookies. But this would be the final summer I found enjoyment in such special blessings of childhood pleasures.

In August the second half of my first year in school began. I was tall for my age. Suddenly I hated my short hair and asked Mama if I could let it grow to a longer length. She agreed quite readily. Like Tata, she encouraged change, as long as they were not harmful in any way, shape or form to our well being. Keeping ourselves clean and neat took top priority. Overalls continued to be my after school wear, but during this past summer I did resort to wearing shorts. The outfits came with a little wrap around removable skirt that a proper young lady could slip into whenever she ventured further then the front door of her home or, as in my case, Mrs. Kreml's front steps.

Classes were numbered 1A and 1B…and it seemed like no time at all had passed for my entry into 1B. I still had Mrs. Walsh as my teacher, but our reading, writing and all our other studies escalated now. By January, when I began 2A, I knew how to write my name quite skillfully and rather beautifully…at least I felt proud of my accomplishments. Reading continued to be a great and most enjoyable challenge. The excitement of Christmas Eve and New Years Eve would continue to stay foremost in my life for years to come. Despite the fact that I would soon be starting second grade, I became that pre-school child again during these holidays. The security I felt in this home was so overwhelming at times, I often wished life would stop exactly where it was. But I knew that was impossible, especially when Tata looked so proud of how well his tree was growing…its strong trunk, the rich green leaves every spring; I knew he felt the same about his family. With all the nurturing love he gave us, I suspected he felt as proud of how well Halina and I were doing in our growing years. No, time dare not stand still. It had to go on.

Second grade introduced me to Miss Metzger and her passion for music. While Mrs. Walsh taught us to sing the Star Spangled Banner, which we did each morning after the Pledge of Allegiance to the flag, that was the extend of our music in first grade. Now, in second grade, all our required subjects, reading, writing, arithmetic, continued on during morning hours. But in the afternoon...Miss Metzger's favorite subject took precedence.

Every afternoon her agenda never changed: class settled at their desk, Miss Metzger closed the school room door, opened the transom a bit wider, as well as the windows in fall and certainly wide open in spring. All of this so our marvelous attempts at learning music could be heard not only through the halls of Hamline, but outdoors as well.

Miss Metzger was a tiny little red head with a voice that belied her stature. When she struck a key on the piano and blew her tuning whistle and raised her arms, the voice that came forth from her throat truly made the hairs on the back of my neck rise. I had never heard anything so marvelous outside the movie theatre or on our radio at home.

She bellowed out and taught us songs so popular during World war I: My Buddy; When Johnny Comes Marching Home Again, K-K-K-Katy ...and Bye, Bye, Blackbird, or my favorite, The Owl and the Pussycat. She adored Stephen Foster music, and we could count on at least one of his songs a day. When she had the entire class going with the enjoyment of Row, Row, Row Your Boat, our laughter filled those halls along with our jovial voices.

Because our home was always filled with so much music, it was never a stranger to me. From the day I was born I heard Mama or Tata singing, and then a radio always played music. Mama sang many of the songs she remembered from her days during the roaring twenties. I sang along with her, these, my first American songs. Then, of course, there were the tunes Tata sang in Polish, which I enjoyed just as much. So I found little trouble engaging and delighting in whatever Miss Metzger offered in second grade. I really hated so see semester 2A and 2B come to a close.

1935 and 1936 brought good things to the world around me, and many bad things as well.

Polio became prevalent in 1935, Mama never again allowed me to play in the water of a turned on fire hydrant. She felt sure that ice cold water hitting those hot summer bodies could easily bring on a bout of Polio. For a time we stopped attending movies as well. Months later Mama finally felt it safe enough to allow that pleasure to resume.

Christmas Eve of '36 was celebrated with a new board game called Monopoly. My cousins and I played with it incessantly whenever we visited at either home. Even as now, I never won.

Now I was old enough to accompany Mama to the beauty parlor every Saturday afternoon. Emily became our new sitter now, but I always felt she was there more for my little sister then for me. After all, I would soon be eight years old. Mama and Tata's outings were changing; they never stayed out as late. Is fact, I think Mama would have preferred not going out at all. It was always Tata who initiated an evening out. Later in life, when Mama and I often had our woman-to-woman chats, she revealed a secret to me. 'Tata was a big flirt. No, I don't think he ever cheated on me. But, if I had not accompanied him to those parties he so enjoyed, who knows. So I dare not let him venture out on those Saturday evenings.' It was during those Saturdays they planned an evening out that I accompanied Mama to the beauty shop.

Tata tended to the bakery store on those afternoons; Halina was much easier to care for now and stayed in the bakery with Tata. I am sure she found the same enjoyment as I did with his stories and singing.

The beauty shop was located in a downstairs basement of a two story flat, just around the corner from where we lived. While I sat quietly in a chair, I marveled at the beauticians ability to perform her wonders with Mama's lovely dark hair. Deep waves, a small bun in the back, then a false matching braid of hair wrapped around Mama's head transformed her image to a queenly look.

After Mama returned from the beauty shop, she always stopped to let Tata know she was home and would soon be downstairs to tend to the store. But first, she had to give her nails their weekly manicure. Mama had lovely long slender fingers. When she began filing each nail to a perfectly round edge that just reached the tip of each finger, I vowed one day I would stop biting my nails. She always allowed me to soak my fingers along with hers in the warm sudsy water, and even pushed my cuticles back as gently as she did hers. The bright red nail polish she applied to her nails looked lovelier on her nails then on my chewed down messy ones, but I still felt special when she applied a coat of polish across my nails. By the end of the weekend, my nails were almost free of the red lacquer, while Mama's seemed to last all week. She always removed her nail polish with a special remover every Friday, just after house cleaning.

Those Saturday evenings, as Mama prepared herself for a fine evening out with Tata, I never grew tired of sitting on the edge of our tub to watch as she applied her Coty's face powder, then wet a little brush and run it over a cake of some magic potion in a little red container and carefully apply it to her lashes and brows. After carefully rubbing a small dab of cream rouge across each cheek and some deep red lipstick unto her lips, that wondrously matched her painted nails, Mama looked as glamorous as any star on the screen. She looked so gloriously feminine that evening as she stood in her finest dress and Tata helped her don a shiny black caracole fur (which is the curly fleece of Astrakhn sheep) in winter time, and slip her polished fingered hands into a matching muff. I thought nothing more beautiful then my mother.

With Mama's penchant for dressing nicely and keeping herself so well-groomed, it was not difficult for everyone else in our household to do the same…especially Tata.

During his work week Tata wore overalls and white shirt. On week-ends, when he and Mama went out or company came to our home, Tata's attire was sharply pressed trousers and always a white starched shirt and tie. Tata's liking for that perfect crease carried back to his days working in the tailor shop. It was not unusual to see him pressing his own trousers on many occasions. That and his shirts starched to perfection were his only demand to complete his outfit of a dark suit and a conservative matching tie. While he wore a cap during the week, the Stetson fedora hats he wore for these special evenings out were blocked and each kept in a separate hat box. The many white shirts in Tata's wardrobe were destined to cause me some consternation when I grew old enough to run errands for Mama.

Being so particular about his shirts, Mama never washed or ironed them. Tata preferred sending them to a Chinese laundry located on 49th. and Ashland. I never gave that laundry much thought, because Mama always picked them up on her way home from the butcher or poultry shop, until that day the job of picking them up was added to my chores.

There were always two places I hated to go...the poultry store where Mama bought fresh chicken for our Sunday dinners, or the duck blood she used for that marvelous Czernina soup. As I mentioned, the smell in that poultry store was enough to turn my taste buds upside-down. Fear of entering the Chinese laundry came about the time I began fourth grade. It was playground gossip that filled me with that fear. Stories of how Chinese men kidnapped women and children and sold them as slaves in China gave me nightmares. I was determined never to step into such a den. When Mama asked me that very first time to pick up Tata's shirts, I felt terror enter my insides. I felt sure I was doomed. Mama would never see me again once I stepped inside that Chinese laundry. I would be carried off to China, never again to see my dear family, friends and country.

When I tried explaining these fears to Mama, she merely raised her brows and said I was being silly, that I should not believe everything I hear from well-meaning friends. She had, after all, dealt with this laundry for years and felt perfectly confident that I would be safe. 'Now go, go. Tata will need a clean shirt this evening.' She urged. I obeyed. Regardless of any fears or trepidation, I could only hope she was right.

When I reached the little shop, I stopped at the front window and peered inside. How dark and gloomy it looked. I inhaled deeply and went to the door. Opening it slowly, I stepped inside. A peculiar smell immediately hit my nostrils; like a mixture of Slatky's lilacs and Mama's scrubbed floor and our musty basement. My legs felt a bit numb as I stepped to the counter and rang a small bell sitting there. This little 'ding', I felt sure, was to summon the evil man who would carry me away. When a skinny little man, with dark rimmed glasses and a wide large toothy smile appeared from behind a curtained doorway, I could only hold my breath and think: 'this is it.' He stood behind the counter directly in front of me. Without a word he reached across the counter and plucked the laundry ticket from my numb fingers and disappeared behind the curtain again. Returning ever so quickly with the package containing Tata's shirts, he asked, in a voice that flowed like honey, how Mama was. I answered, fine. He smiled and thanked me, wished me a good day and said to give his best to Mama. I knew Mama paid him monthly, so there was no exchange of money. Suddenly, it occurred to me as he was speaking, my fears melted away like butter beneath a warm sun. Mama had been right, and as I said good-bye, I felt rather foolish having those earlier silly fears.

When I returned home and told Mama about my conversation with the Chinese man and how quickly my fears dissipated, she was not surprised. ' Mr. Wang is a very nice man . Always polite, and very hard working.' Then she reminded me again, as she often would, that I must learn to accept the different people in this country. Mama and Tata rarely prejudged anyone. 'Fear, rather then hate, is what we should feel for evil people.' Mama once said. 'And then you must be strong enough to stay away from them.' Which, I found out later in life, is sometimes much more difficult to do then say. When I heard a song from the musical, South Pacific, that children have to be taught to hate...it reminded me of Mama and Tata's teachings. Tata believed in the golden rule of doing unto others as we would have them do unto us. Unfortunately, too many others in our world found hate a simpler, albeit not a safer or better, alternative.

Mama's quest to continue my cultural education came in the form piano lessons. They were about to become part of my life the summer of my seventh year. I will never forget the day that old upright was delivered to our home. A second hand dark mahogany, the delivery men knew immediately this large piece of furniture would never make it through the turn in that hallway between porch and upstairs kitchen. But Tata was determined to have that piano in our living room. After much measuring, all the men decided the only way to do that was to remove the window in the back bedroom. That would leave an opening wide enough for the piano. So out it came. And up through that opening, the piano was hoisted by rope and man power. All I could think of as I watched the long drawn out operation was that I had better not disappoint Mama and Tata with my piano lessons as I had with tap dancing lessons.

My piano teacher was a young woman by the name of Miss Kraszny. A delightfully easy going teacher, her soft spoken voice made piano lessons enjoyable. Unfortunately she could not convey the same enjoyment to practicing each and every day. I hated to practice. How I ever managed to get through three years of lessons is a wonder. Mama thought I was doing so well, and Tata seemed to receive such great enjoyment when I played the piano for him on Sunday afternoons or those evenings during the week, when his work ended earlier. Perhaps I felt terrible guilt, in seeing them so content and my hating those practice hours. This was definitely not going the way I had hoped. I thought Mama herself would finally see, or hear, that I really was not enjoying those sessions. No, of course not, because truth be known, I did enjoy playing for the sheer pleasure of it. It was the practice, practice, practice I detested. So something had to be done, and I could not come out openly and say anything. The fear of hurting Mama's feeling kept me from it. No, it had to be something more subtle. Something that would make her feel sorry for me.

Parental authority was not taken lightly when I was a child growing up at this time. Most adults, or anyone in uniform, were considered a high enough force to be reckoned with. If we did not obey, there was always the threat of 'the reformatory.' A building we passed on our week-end trips to Aunt Isabelle's house. A rather austere looking red brick building, it sat behind a very high and rather ugly metal fence. Mama never hesitated to point it to me each time we drove past. 'If you do not listen and obey your elders' (which took in a great deal of people) 'or if you break the law in any way, this is where you will spend the remainder of your life.' Not a pleasant thought at all to a child…especially a child who found so much comfort and love in her home. I found it much simpler and consoling to behave then suffer such consequences. Of course, much later in life, I learned that the reformatory was more a housing facility for orphaned and neglected children then those who misbehaved. Still, this was an era of truant officers, and gangsters exchanging gun power with officers of the law. So I hardly wanted to end up in their company.

But the day finally arrived when I had to make Mama aware just how much I detested practicing those scales and the mundane notes that had absolutely no likeness to any likeable music. Plus, the structured lessons were beginning to grind on my nerves as well. It was time to get my life back. I felt I had accomplished quite a bit in those three years. Two recitals plus a gold medal for scales well done, what more could I possibly do?

Yet I dreaded telling Mama openly about my feelings. So in that rash moment of unthinking consequences, I thought of a horribly different way to communicate my feelings.

One summer day, after waking early in the morning and preparing for the day, while Mama was already downstairs busy in the bakery shop, I decided it was time to rub the tops of my fingers, just below the knuckles, until they almost bled raw. Surely after Mama saw my sore fingers she would not make me practice. What's more, she would know I did this to let her know how much I hated practicing. I managed to rub only one finger on each hand…the burning was almost more then I could bear. I immediately went downstairs. Mama was in the kitchen washing up a few breakfast dishes. I showed her the raw spots on my fingers and told her I could not possibly practice the piano for at least a week…or perhaps never again, since the thought of practicing drove me to doing this to my fingers. Perhaps at that moment Mama may have taught me a bit insane as she bent over and examined each finger carefully. She sighed deeply and shook her head as she stood and looked down at me. I did not know if I should feel guilt for the sad look in her eyes, or fear of the tightly pursed lips.

'Why did you not come and tell me how much you hated playing the piano.' The pain in her voice made my stomach go topsy-turvey. I suddenly realized I had done something much worse then mutilate my fingers. How terribly childish the act had been, and I, the one Mama counted on to be the wisest of her two daughters. 'But I do love playing the piano.' As if Mama's knowing this would amend what I had done. ' Only the practicing Mama, that is the only thing I wish to give up…' My remorseful voice begged. 'I am sure I would enjoy spending hours playing that music that I enjoy and not what is expected of me.' Oh, how I hoped this would reassure Mama that I never meant to cause her this much pain. That I truly appreciated all she and Tata did for me in their quest to expand my musical horizons.

Mama clasped her hand together tightly and pressed them over her pursed lips. 'Then, we may as well stop the piano lessons. But I want you to remember one thing: the most important is that you never again be so afraid to talk to me before you do something this foolish. That you felt a need to hurt yourself in this way because you were afraid to tell me…it makes me sad. I am always here to listen to you and what you want from life. It may not be what I dream for you, but I am always willing to listen to your side. The piano lessons are only a small part of what you like or do not like in your life. I hope you will continue to enjoy what you have learned so far. But remember this little one, things that we start in our life cannot always be set aside as easily as piano lessons and practicing. Many times you will find the lessons of life much more difficult…and the practicing to get it right, even more difficult. It may take a great amount of courage and strength to continue in those things you may not like to do. I hope you never give up as easily with other things in your life as you have with your piano lessons and practicing.

My lessons did stop. And I did continue playing the piano with much enjoyment. All in all, it seemed to work out perfectly. During her final visit to our home, Miss Krasny announced she was getting married and moving away. I do not know if Mama ever told her what I did, but Miss Krasny encouraged me on that last day to continue playing the piano, if only for my own enjoyment. Perhaps this was the best lesson ever I learned from her, to please myself and not those around me. Nonetheless, Mama and Tata also seemed satisfied with whatever music I played for that self-enjoyment. They never once complained on money spent for those lessons or the fact that I did not live up to any great expectations they may have had. They seemed perfectly content that I played at all, and as best I could. If they thought otherwise, it never showed on their face or in their voice as they sat and smiled and complimented me each time I played the piano, especially when I did so just for them.

Mama's words would guide me throughout my entire life. I found many of lifes lessons quite hard, but never again did I give up or give in so easily to those difficulties. If success did not always come, I at least knew I had given my all to trying.

When it came to housekeeping, Mama was not as lenient. To her this was an education as important as learning to read and write the English language. Thankfully, it did become a chore I rather enjoyed.

I became part of the Friday ritual of cleaning our flat during my second summer vacation. My lessons began with dusting and scrubbing my bedroom floor. The following summer Mama added our large kitchen and her bedroom. Since I learned from early childhood that clothing or wet bath towels were never left on the floor…or that dishes waiting to be washed never sat in the sink for hours, or especially over night, learning to clean our flat in Mama's proper manner was not difficult. Mama's philosophy was: when dust and clutter begin to pile up one has a tendency to grow lazier and lazier; or: if you want an orderly life, learn to keep an orderly home. With these beliefs, our flat may have looked rumpled at times, but never in such disarray that we had to, so to speak, crawl over misplaced items. I never really realized there was such a thing as an unkept home until I visited Elaine's home one day. Clothing tossed carelessly over chairs, unwashed dishes piled up in the sink. When I used the bathroom in her home, wet towels heaped in one corner and smelling of mildew made me cringe a bit. When I reiterated this unpleasant experience to Mama her defense of the untidy flat surprised me. 'Perhaps Elaine's mother never had anyone to teach her better habits. Now her habits are being passed down to Elaine. Just remember one thing, seeing how differently they live does not mean we are any better then they are…only neater. I have known some very high-class people who cared or knew little of keeping order in their home.' Of course, later I realized Mama may have

125

been referring to Dr. Kalinowski's wife. Mama's broad outlook did teach me to keep an open mind on how differently everyone lived. So too, in this frame of mind I began to look upon those children in school who arrived unwashed and dressed in scraggly or unpressed clothing quite differently. I soon discovered they had the same dreams and desires as any other child beginning their education. Only theirs perhaps taking longer to obtain because of parents who cared so little to listen to their voice. I felt blessed indeed to come home to a flat clean and smelling of freshly baked cookies. Mama, having gone through such difficult time in her childhood, always reminded me to include the unfortunate children in my evening prayers.

Friday was, by far, the best day to return home from school. Not only did it mean a long week-end of family fun but it was the day our flat sparkled with clean freshness. That smell of Fels-Naphta soap as I stepped through the door of the back porch was the first indication of Mama's busy cleaning day. Climbing those clean steps that led to our kitchen door told me she had worked very hard that day. The scent was especially strong on a cold winter day. When the senses come alive in temperatures that turn noses red and color cheeks pink, walking through that door unto the porch the change in smelling something different was instant. If it snowed or rained on Friday, Mama had old copies of Tata's Polish paper spread across the porch floor, the small hall leading to our kitchen, and of course on the kitchen floor as well. Just below the telephone, that hung in the hallway next to the kitchen door, Mama laid out several sheets of newspaper. This was where we all had to stop to remove our galoshes. I cannot remember how many times the sudden ring of that black phone made me jump as I bent over to slip out of my galoshes. Before I was old enough to reach that phone, I had to open the door and yell out to Mama that the phone was ringing…just in case she did not hear it. Our phone number stays imbedded in my mind: YA7-6219. Mama hurried to answer the ring, shooing me inside the warm kitchen, and then conversing with the caller.

I continued my undressing in the large warm kitchen. Mittens tucked in my coat pocket, off came the cap, coat and scarf, which I would carefully place over the back of a chair...until that day Felix put up a lower rod in one of the closets so Halina and I could hang up or get down our own clothing.

The entire flat smelled divine. Not only the smell of soap and dusting oil, but the incense Mama discovered just about the time I started second grade. Now, every Friday after cleaning our flat, she would place the small pyramid shaped incense cone on a little copper plate that sat on the dining room table. Putting lit match to the tip, Mama held it there until the tip grew bright red. She blew out the match and stood there waiting, for that little ribbon of smoke the soon began its climb. The ribbon of smoke almost reached the chandelier above the table, its woodsy scent mingling in a delicious medley with the oil and soap. To this day I equate any one of those scents with fresh clean surroundings.

After greeting Mama and Halina with a kiss, I hurried to the bathroom to wash my hands before going back downstairs to visit with Tata in the bakery. He would either be waiting on a customer or helping Miecheck in baking sweet rolls or bread for Saturday sales and delivery. Some days I might even find him having a cup of coffee and a slice of rye bread smeared with bacon grease. I always hoped for the latter. Tata always shared whatever he was eating with me. That bacon grease with little bits of crisp bacon tasted marvelously decadent on that rye bread with its crisp crust.

When I began helping Mama with her housekeeping, she always thanked me for easing her burden. The lessons I learned from her were far more rewarding then her thanks. I would have guesses she appreciated my well accomplished tasks without her saying so. I rather enjoyed this grown-up task, especially since it always gave me a chance to tease my baby sister.

Halina used to sit on the sidelines, so to speak, as I began scrubbing that large kitchen floor. Kitchen table and chairs were moved to one side of the room because scrubbing that floor always began near the bathroom. Before I was assigned the bathroom into my Friday cleaning, Mama always had that clean before I began on the kitchen. After doing that area, table and chairs went back, and I would start at the far side of the kitchen, near the dining room archway, where Halina sat watching me.

She sat there so entranced by what I was doing, I often wondered if she envied me or felt relief that she was not old enough to help. I never found out which.

As soon as I began scrubbing the floor at that doorway, my stories began. They were the usual fairy tales that Mama or Tata always told me. But it was one I made up myself that Halina always begged to hear.

'You know,' I began my tale,' Mama and Tata kidnapped me from a group of gypsy travelers. I was just a little girl then. My real mother had golden red hair, just like mine. My real father was tall and sang and told stories just like the Tata I have now...but my gypsy father had black curly hair and a beard down to his waist. My real parents were terribly poor, and always very hungry. When they stopped at our bakery that one day and saw all the fine bread and cakes for sale, they wanted everything...but had no money. And so they traded me for all that bread and cake. Mama and Tata were so happy to get me. They always wanted a blue-eyed blond baby girl...and here I was, theirs for the taking. Later, Mama and Tata found out my gypsy mother and father were the king and queen of the gypsies. So that makes me a real princess. That also means you are not really my sister. Which you can well see by the color of my hair and my eyes, which are just like my gypsy mother's. Next year I will have you scrubbing every floor in this place. And if you do a good job, when my real parents come for me, I will reward you with diamonds and pearls.'

Halina would sit and listen quietly. Her large brown eyes wide, her mind probably wondering if my story were true or not. No matter how many times I told her this story, I felt sure she was eager to run downstairs and ask Mama or Tata about the truth of it. But she dare not step on the floor while it was wet, and I took my time so that she might contemplate the story and our differences in hair and eye coloring. We were, after all, as different as night and day. She dark eyed with dark hair and very petite; while I was a strawberry-blond with blue-green eyes and definitely not petite. Halina also favored Mama's charming little pug nose. I inherited Tata's slavic features. It was not until my later years that I began to appreciate this gift he gave me. When I finally realized I was rather pretty, it was then I began to lose my shyness and the outside world looked rosier.

In those years from first to fifth grade, Halina and I had a very close sisterly relationship. We played together, walked to school together, and attended the Saturday matinee movies at Crystal Theatre on 49th and Ashland. These were the 'serial' days of Flash Gordon, Rin-Tin-Tin or Tom Mix or any other weekly movie-chapter that pulled children to those Saturday matinees. How could any of us miss those exciting serials, let alone Betty Boop or The Three Stooges.

At this time there were two movie theaters located in the vicinity of our neighborhood. Crystal Theatre on 49th, east of Ashland, was the closest. The other one was Peoples Show on 47th, west of Ashland. Since Mama felt we were not old enough to cross busy Ashland Avenue on our own, we attended Crystal Theatre.

It was a small movie house. Inside, a center block of seats, sat about twenty rows deep and fifteen seats across. To the side, against each wall, from front to back, were two seats in each row. Halina and I always sat in those side seats. I found it less congested with Saturday afternoon noise and the all too frequent spitballs that came from unruly boys.

On one particular Saturday, as we sat watching the movie of the week, I heard someone grunt and scoot into the seat directly behind ours. I thought it was another child, until the man leaned over and whispered an obscene word in my ear. My body froze. I no longer cared what was on the screen. We had to leave, quickly....I knew that much. I was about nine years old at the time and with Halina three years younger, I felt it was up to me to get us home safely.

I knew the man was drunk. I could smell his liquor infested breath. That terrified me all the more. When Tata had too much to drink he was always in a laughing playful mood. Mama said we were lucky. Some men, she added, grew violent and hit their wives and children whenever they drank. Perhaps even killing them. I could only think the worst with the stranger sitting behind us now.

I leaned over and told Halina we had to get home—now, and fast. She never questioned my decision as I took her hand and hurried her through the dark theatre to the front door and outdoors. Since we attended the early afternoon movies, full daylight was still with us. As I pulled my sister along side of me I turned several times to see if the man had followed us. I knew instantly the scruffy messy looking man hurrying to catch up to us was the same one who accosted us in the theatre. The smirk on his unshaven face, his dirty clothes and unruly hair and what he whispered to us in the theatre was evil personified to a little girl who knew very little about such evil. I had heard about the terrible things that happened to children who were kidnapped and often killed. That knowledge made my fear grow large at this moment.

As he drew closer I began to again smell the liquor that engulfed him like a dirty blanket. He continued his obscene language and said such things as: 'I like what you have between your legs...I can make you feel good...stop and talk to me, I won't hurt you.' The chicken store was on the corner, where we would turn left and head toward Loomis. As the man rambled on I leaned toward Halina and said. 'Just hold on tightly to my hand and walk fast. When we turn the corner, run.' Which we did. As fast as we could. Not until we reached the corner of Wishniewski's tavern did I dare stop us and turn to see if the man followed as well.

There he stood, way back, clear on the other side of Laflin Street, his arm raised in anger. He had either been too drunk or too stunned to follow and stopped dead in his tracks. I kept holding Halina's hand. We were a bit winded, and very tired. I, more from fright then anything. When we reached our bakery, I made sure we went into the store first, where I knew Mama would be clerking. When I told her what had happened, she said : 'Bocze Kochany'; which translates to 'Dear God'. Then she knelt down and embraced both of us. Standing again, she took us by the hand and led us to the baking area and told Tata about our terrible encounter. He immediately ran out to look for the man, but never found him. For a long time after we were not allowed to go to the movies. When Mama finally consented to Saturday afternoon matinees again, she and Tata felt Peoples Show was probably a safer place. More people attended that theatre, and there were always shoppers going and coming from stores on Ashland. Nothing like that ever happened again. Later, when Olympia Theatre opened up as well on Ashland, Crystal theatre finally had to close its doors because of the competition from two larger theatres.

Mama and Tata loved movies as well. But they preferred the large movie theatres in the Loop. Not only did these theatres show movies but had live stage shows between the movie, news and cartoon. Comedians, dancers, singers, were what Tata especially enjoyed. The first movie I remember seeing at a downtown theatre was an amazing movie called, 'The Good Earth.'

As for myself, the radio remained a good companion for many years. After school, on rainy days or days to icy cold for venturing outdoors and even after attending a movie on either Saturday or Sunday, Halina and I hurried home to listen to our favorite radio programs. My memory is still filled with The Aldrich Family, Amos 'n' Andy, Ripleys Believe It or Not, The Bob Hope Show, Death Valley Days, Grand Central Station…our choices were boundless. Broadcasts that made me laugh, brought me alive with glorious music and stirred my imagination beyond the wildest in those years of radio.

Sunday continued to be family time. By the time I was ready to begin fifth grade Tata now thought nothing of closing the bakery all week-end and take all of us to the Indiana Sand Dunes. The trips were usually one day excursions. The picnic lunches Mama for our picnics were always scrumptious treats of roast chicken, sausage, rye bread, dill pickles and jars of tea. Spending a day on the beach, whether at the dunes or Lake Michigan, we found running through the water and the sand, then sitting down to this fine meal, made our day complete.

When the weather became too cool for excursions to the beach, a drive to Jackson Park and a walk around the lagoon another favorite outing. Tata would rent a boat and row us around the little island. But there is one autumn week-end I will always remember as most special and unusual.

One of Tata's and Mama's friends from the Polish Choir had now retired and bought himself a small farm in the outskirts of Chicago. We visited them quite often, just for the joy of feeding the chickens, eating a meal of freshly laid eggs and watching the cows get milked. Tata seemed quite at home on this farm. As to the rest of us city folk, especially Halina and myself, we were fascinated by all of it. I clearly remember that one taste of milk I had one day. Fresh from a just milked cow, it tasted so warm and creamy. Mama became quite upset when she found out I drank a glass of this milk. She said such milk was most unhealthy, that the one she bought in bottle at the store was far safer for us. Of course, we never got the cream taste from bottled milk delivered to us each morning. Mama always poured that off for her and Tata's coffee.

While visiting this farm one week, we were invited to attend a barn dance. I was almost nine years old, and although I enjoyed visiting the farm and seeing the farm animals, I had little desire to sleep there over-night. This old farm house had no indoor bathroom facilities. Bad enough to use the outhouse during the day, I dreaded the idea of going outdoors early in the morning to use that facility...or worse, in the middle of the night. Luckily, a chamber pot was provided to each of us for night time use, which of course was much better then going outdoors into a dark night and the outhouse, where the smell was disgusting. And thankfully, the thick quilt I slept under was warm and cozy enough to keep me asleep all night.

The barn dance was held on the second evening of our stay. I got to wear my favorite overalls and a flannel shirt supplied by Tata's friend. The dance was held in a large red barn about a half hours drive from where we were staying. By the time we arrived at the barn the sound of fiddlers music and laughter already filled the clear crisp autumn air.

A man standing at the barn entrance stamped the back of my hand with a red number as we entered the barn. If I had to leave the barn for any reason, he knew by that stamped number who reentered as an invited guest. The music was lively...and quite unlike any I had ever heard before. Everyone, including Mama and Tata, danced through the night, especially when the music resembled those Polish polkas they loved dancing to. This would be the last autumn month we got to visit this farm. Mr. Adamowski, the man who always invited us out, came down with leukemia that winter. He died the following spring. I remember Tata telling Mama what a wonderful wake his friend had. Mama shied away from wakes or funerals for a number of years after Babsha died. But Tata always enjoyed a good Polish wake.

They were big, noisy and there was always an abundance of good food. In fact, Tata enjoyed them so much he attended many wakes without even knowing the deceased. Perhaps, and this is only my observation, he missed his socializing and found this a fair substitute. Just as he always enjoyed mushroom hunting with his best chum Mr. Chmielewski.

At this time 87th seemed a far off place from where we lived. Then it was a heavily wooded area with an skirting of farms. I enjoyed going along with Tata and his friend just for the pleasure of picking the wild sunflowers that grew here. Tata was an expert mushroom hunter. He always came home with several brown bags filled with the delectable morsals. Along with onions, Mama also added mushrooms to just about everything she cooked.

Summer days of family outings, movies, the radio, errands and chores. Rolly-Polly, Hopscotch and roller skating. Dressed in either overalls or shorts, my hair quite long by the end of '38, it never took me long to prepare for the day. There were kittens to play with when my friends were not available and as much as I enjoyed attending school, I hated to see every summer come to a close.

By 1938 the depression eased further and the number of out of work people on relief dropped further. Tata was shocked when Chmielewski told him he heard that Hitler was named Man of the Year. They read too many stories in the Polish paper to know this was not the man everyone supposed him to be.

Mama was not too happy to hear that Uncle George and Aunt Isabelle were talking about moving to California, where the job market was more plentiful. On this Fourth of July, Tata, for the very first time, celebrated his birthday and bought fireworks for the special double occasion. He became a little boy again as he lit up fireworks that flew into the sky, and joined in our laughter at those quiet ones that simply wiggled around on the sidewalk. Halina and I were only allowed to hold sparklers, which we twisted and turned in front of us and watched with fascination as dainty little sparkling little stars danced about haphazardly.

That Christmas Eve of '38 Halina finally guessed who Santa really was. This would be Tata's final year of dressing in his Santa outfit, and our final one to carrying out a bucket of water for the reindeer. My newest added chore of '38 would be helping Tata with his evening task of loading his delivery truck with bakery goods for morning delivery.

Tata kept at least two dozen large wooden trays in his truck. Every evening he would bring them into the baking area, take out his order book and, depending on each grocers order, begin to fill each wooden tray with sweet rolls and buns. Once filled, he covered each tray with a clean damp cloth, then carried each tray back to the garage and loaded his truck. I began helping with this ritual every Friday evening.

I was always fascinated with what went on in the baking area. The golden bread, the marvelous sweet rolls so painstakingly rolled and filled to perfection, and the chance to help Tata get his truck ready for the delivery of these tasty cakes and buns. As he filled each wooden tray, I covered it with the damp towel and carried the tray out to his truck. Afterwards Tata always rewarded my hard work with an egg drink He would poke a hole in one end of a fresh egg, hand it to me and instruct me to put it to my mouth, lean my head back and suck hard until the egg came out of that hole. The taste of a raw egg seemed marvelously different to me. As a child curious with new delights, I rather enjoyed it. Obviously Salmonella was an unheard of thing back then.

By the end of '38 Halina and I had made our First Holy Communion and, shortly after, I was confirmed. Except for the one prayer I always said for Babsha, my evening prayers were now said in English. So many evenings, as I lay in bed contemplating how happy I was, I added a little prayer that this simple perfect life would never change.

Funny, those things we wish never to change, do; those we wish would change, do not. For now, with fall and winter just around the corner, life was an unchanging happy place from my point of view.

Mama and Tata spent fall and winter evenings reading their Polish paper and listening to the radio. A Polish station played the music they enjoyed and broadcast all the latest news in Polish as well. For Halina and myself there was nothing better then the radio programs we preferred, which many times caused discontent for us when Tata had top priority to his Polish station. So that Christmas Eve of '38, our surprise gift was a radio for the room that was once called our 'playroom'. Now it was a room used for reading and soon for listening to our radio. Although the kitchen table would forever be the ideal cozy place for homework, the seclusion of our very own room with our very own little radio was a treat as welcomed as an ice cream cone on a warm day.

I paid little mind to the news of the day or the hour. If any changes were coming, I was not aware of them. Winter continued after Christmas, and soon the new year would begin. I felt peacefully blessed with my home, my neighborhood and the world around me.

1939 THROUGH 1941

The first change came in school. In January I started sixth grade. That meant I would now be considered an upper-classman. And my last three years in grammar school would be held on the second floor of Hamline. Also, I would now begin changing classes between each period. School still started at nine A.M.. Science, art classes and physical education were added to our studies. Apparently the school board felt everyone did enough running around on the school yard in grades one through five, and so the wait until sixth grade to begin a class of indoor exercises to help keep us fit. All of the classes were divided to fit into that scheduled day of nine to three, with forty-five minutes for lunch, and two fifteen minute recess periods. I was growing up, quickly. As was the neighborhood around me.

Walking to Sherman Parks library was a delightful journey. All of those trees, planted long before I was born, were pleasingly sturdy and tall now. The eight block walk to the library, which I began doing on my own just about the Spring in 1939, felt enchantingly lovely. It also opened my eyes to how everything was beginning to change. There were more all brick homes, bungalows to be exact, being built. Traffic on Loomis Street was getting heavier…it was no longer safe to roller-skate on this street. Still, this was my compact little world of safety and warmth. Walking beneath those tall trees in early spring, when buds were only beginning to show, the walk from 49th and Loomis to 55th and Racine, filled me with something I found difficult to express or tune into as a child. Now I realize that feeling was pride and contentment. Seeing mothers with their children strolling through Sherman Park, I know now they too must have felt what I did. Certainly none of use realized then that one day this serenity of peace and safety we took so for granted would be gone.

I looked to summer vacation more this year then ever before. Oh, I still enjoyed going to school every day…except for the physical education class, and sometimes math, all classes enticed my yearning to learn more. Gym classes were my worst nightmare come true. After my short stint with tap-dancing lessons and finding out I was definitely not athletically inclined, I barely made a passing grade in Phys.Ed. . I was never so glad and thankful to get back to reading and writing after a period of gym class.

Tata was driving a large gold colored DeSoto now, and that spring he had Felix help him build a bench for us to sit on in front of the bakery. The sturdy piece, whose legs were cemented into the ground, sat facing Tata's tree. Tata painted it gray the first year, but decided on a dark green the years after. Shaded by Tata's ever growing tree, it became a favorite place to sit at any time of the year; in the spring, summer and fall to read, visit with neighbors—who often stopped here to chat with Mama, or when Rosemary and I sat down to rest between roller-skating trips around the block. In the winter it was mostly a place to sit and rest between snow shoveling or breaking and sweeping the ice that covered our sidewalk.

Winter's were often ferocious in Chicago. Because of the large baking oven downstairs, the kitchen there was actually cozier then the one in the flat upstairs. But this year Tata decided to purchase 'storm windows'. Heavy framed glass windows that Tata installed against our bedroom and living room windows every spring thereafter. He would struggle precariously on a wooden ladder, placing each storm window against the existing window. Ice would no longer cover our inside windows and they seemed to keep much of the cold winter wind at bay as well. But they were not full-proof. Sitting on the radiator in the living room, I could still feel a chill coming in from the outside. On those days, when temperatures dropped below zero, nothing could keep the puckered lips of that whistling cold winter wind from finding some small openings in our storm windows. When spring came, the effort of getting those storm windows down was as great as when Tata put them up. Only now Mama stood at the bottom of the ladder, ready to assist as Tata climbed down carefully, slowly…storm window in one hand, his other hanging tightly to the ladder, Mama grabbing the window as soon as Tata reached three or four rungs from the bottom. Then began the spring cleaning…windows first, everything else following.

Easter of this year brought my Catholicism to a new level. Since Catechism lessons and my very first confession, as sure as every breath I took, I felt certain I was doomed to Hell if I did not live up to what the good sisters taught me, or follow all those rules preached by the priest who visited our Saturday class once a month. But there was also a natural interest in stories about saints as well. Not that I could ever follow in any of their footsteps, or even want to, but certainly my efforts to be a better Catholic began this Easter. Confession and all those recited penance prayers helped ease my childhood transgressions. Attending Sunday mass became a must in my quest for heavenly joy in the afterlife. Yet I could not help but remember the time someone broke into our flat and stole all of Tata and Mama's treasured possessions; or that terrible man at Crystal Theatre who surely meant to harm Halina and me. If it was so simple to be good and so simple to find forgiveness, why did such evil exist? I had no answers. I began to contemplate asking Mama the whys of this complicated question—but that summer Mama became quite ill.

Her first spell came while she was shopping for a new housedress in a little shop on Ashland Avenue. While in the dressing room of this shop, she had a fainting spell. A clerk found our phone number in Mama's purse and immediately phoned Tata. He wasted no time in driving to the store and bringing Mama home. That was the first time she went to see Dr. Nowak, a young family physician just beginning his practice.

At first I thought perhaps Mama's illness came about because she too asked herself those same questions I had. Who had been so evil to take all her treasures? But it was not that. Mama had resigned herself to that loss, I knew this when I heard her telling Mrs. Kreml that Dr. Nowak diagnosed her dizziness and fainting spell to an early onset of menopause. Of course, I felt confident that this doctor would make everything right again with Mama's health. But from her middle thirties, health problems resulting from menopause would plague Mama the rest of her life. Hers resulted in a most sever case of osteoporosis that literally crippled her in later years. Regardless, she remained stoic through all of it...from beginning to end. After this first episode, Mama shied away from crowded places. If she went shopping, it would always be early in the morning, before stores became crowded with too many people. Still, she had more days of feeling good in these early years of menopause, and never allowed her bad days to keep her inactive. It was this early illness and my determination not to burden Mama with too many of my problems that actually helped me mature and grow up more quickly.

Just before summer vacation of 1939, Miss Cummings, our art teacher, assigned Rosemary and me to an art project of drawing posters. Rosemary was not too thrilled on doing any sort of drawings, but for me, it was exciting. Any kind of drawing interested me. Apparently that interest showed itself in my poster, for shortly after Miss Cummings asked me if I might consider talking some art classes that were being offered at the Art Institute in Chicago's loop. Although I had no desire to be an artist, a dress designer perhaps, or a window decorator in a department store like Marshall Field, but not the kind of artist whose wonders were displayed at the Art Museum. Rosemary and I visited the Art Institute once or twice during class trips. Of course I found the paintings enchanting and lovely. I felt I could never come any where near to being as good an artist. Still, I would give the lessons a try. Unfortunately I was much too young to realize this chance of exploring or extending my talents came as a marvelous gift.

Lessons were not on a one to one basis. Students, of all ages, filled a large auditorium which was located in the art institute. From a stage, a teacher instructed us on canvas preparation, structure, colors, etc. The class was held once a week, every Saturday, and would go on for at least one year. After four classes, and still unable to grasp any of the instructions, I began to quickly lose sight of what the instructor was trying to convey. But if I was too young to enter this window and seize this moment of opportunity, I did learn one thing. The teacher emphasized over and over that a good artist always looks at the world around him not only with open eyes, but with an open mind as well. Little by little I began doing this, and eventually really became aware on how everything around me had changed.

I also began to appreciate all the new people that now entered my life as well.

Emily still sat with us whenever Mama and Tata went out on Saturday evening, which was not too often now. But on those Saturdays that she did sit with us, Emily and I had some helpful conversations after Halina was asleep.

I say helpful in the sense that it helped me better understand my growing maturity. As much as Mama and I talked, it would only be in my late teens that she grew more comfortable in discussing any kind of womanly functions or sexual behavior. Hence, now that I was hearing talk on the playground of those changes that began in a young girls body around my age, or how babies were made, I began growing curious as to the truth of all this talk. The first time I approached Mama about the changes, she said I was still too young to know about how babies were made, but did agree to send out for a special little booklet from Kotex that would explain everything to me about menstruation.. Without a doubt the booklet was helpful, and better then no explanation at all. Emily explained everything else in full detail…from the beginning of a menstrual cycle through how babies were made and brought into the world. Our talks enlightened me enough that I never had to ask Mama those embarrassing questions again.

I was old enough to visit friends who lived blocks away from Loomis. As long as I was home for supper, and on week-end evenings with family, I found all new friendships quite interesting. What was most fascinating, that just as Emily dreamed, most every new girl friend I met, their dreams were similair. Yes, I had my movie star crushes, just as anyone other girl my age, but marriage? Hardly. Most of my dreams of the future did not include a man. I was caught between putting together those amazing window displays at Carsons or Fields, or perhaps becoming a reporter and working for the Chicago Tribune. How much more exciting any of these dreams then those Emily and my new friends talked about. Of course, Emily's dreams did become reality. But fate, unknown to me at this time, would render me much the same.

Alice and Frances were two sisters I met one morning on my way to school during September of 1939. Frances had just stepped outdoors with a little girl who apparently was about to start first grade. Her name was Anna. 'Look, this little girl is going to school and she is not crying.' I stopped and smiled at both of them. 'Would you like to walk with me?' I asked Anna, and looked up to Frances for approval. 'How nice, would you like that Anna?' Frances asked the little girl. Anna sobbed and nodded and my friendship with this family began. That fall I visited with them a few times a week and met Alice, who was younger then Frances. Alice sounded like Emily, always wishing and hoping to meet a fine man and get married. She was preparing for the big event by stocking a hope chest with linens, pots and pans, and anything else that would prepare her for that big day. Frances was married to a man who worked at the stockyards. He was never at home when I visited. They had two children. Anna was the oldest and Mary, the youngest. Whenever I visited with them, we usually sat on the front steps of their two flat home. I never stepped inside their home until the following spring, when little Mary died. And again, I realized how cruel life and reality could be.

That great sadness I felt when Babsha died and felt sure would never end, did of course dissipate with time. Thanks much to my loving family who helped see me through those sad days. When Aunt Isabelle and Uncle George packed up children and goods and moved to California, I should have realized this another clue that I could not be protected all my life from that reality that life changes constantly. That it was not always a garden filled with sweet smelling flowers. Like those sweet flowers that eventually withered away in cold dreary fall, so too did our lives change and begin anew with another garden.

Aunt Isabelle wrote and told Mama of their terrible hot journey through western desert country. How they had to resort to purchasing a block of ice and putting it on the back seat between Herby and Madaline so that they might stay cool. But once in California, my Aunt concluded her letter, the weather was clear and cool and not nearly as humid as Chicago. And so I put to rest my sadness of perhaps never seeing my cousins again.

At least they were happy, so I should be happy for them as well. Loomis Street was now Loomis Boulevard, with heavier traffic that took away much of the quiet solitude we had sitting on our green bench. St. Augustine also had a school added to its parish. It accommodated all the new families of German heritage that were added to the melting pot of our neighborhood. The Irish and St. Rose of Lima Church would soon follow. With Mama feeling ill so much of the time now, Tata talked of closing the bakery. I could not even imagine that kind of change in my life. I was glad it was only talk, for now.

While my hair continued to grow longer, Rosemary decided to cut hers. We still preferred shopping on Ashland Avenue to the Loop. With two large department stores, Goldblatt Brothers and Meyer Brothers, and an array of little stores, our choices were almost comparable to downtown shopping. Stores opened at nine A.M. and closed at six and were never opened on Sunday. When Rosemary came calling that last Saturday of shopping before school started again, she shocked me with her very, very short hair. She said her mother just about 'killed her' when she saw the long hair gone. I thought the short hair looked rather attractive on Rosemary. Just as Rosemary was tall and slim, her face was rather long and thin; the short hair added fullness to her face. I told her I loved the new look. 'Well, my mother did too after awhile.' Rosemary said, 'and, after my grandma told me my mother had done exactly the same thing once, I didn't feel so bad.'

We had a marvelous time shopping that day.

August was hot and humid. The influx of Irish families to our neighborhood would bring me my first taste of falling in love. But on this day all I had on my mind was searching for new sheet music at Vitaks Music Store. Now that I played the piano for my own enjoyment, my preference ran from Strauss waltzes, which Mama and Tata enjoyed hearing and to the popular music of the day: Me and My Shadow; 'S Wonderful, Lover Come Back To Me, Embraceable You, I Found a Million Dollar Baby, and so many more that made it most difficult to choose simply one sheet of music. But Mama gave me only enough money for one purchase at Vitaks. Luckily, the Chicago Tribune also carried a new song on the back page of the funnies, at least once a month. One of my very favorite songs from that back page was Ebb Tide. Or, if I merely wanted the words to a song the 5 & 10 cent store carried three page sheets of those most popular songs, for five cents a copy.

As I look back now, the changes crept up on all of was rather unnoticed by most, especially the very young. We accepted them rather matter-of-factly, going along with the flow, so to speak. As one becomes older, we begin to ponder why this or that is happening, and then we begin to question those changes. The question most asked, what consequences do these changes bring?

September meant going forward to a new beginning in school. A fresh season of autumn, leaves getting dressed in their new colors of gold and red. Most of the time a season that meant all those wonderful holidays were just around the corner. This year September first brought unexpected and unwelcome news into all our lives. Hitler invaded Poland on this day. On September third France and Great Britain declared war on Germany.

I remember Mama's tears that morning as she and Tata talked about the invasion. Mr. Chmielewski visited with Tata that evening and their conversation about the war brought more tears to Mama's eyes. Talking about my new friends, Alice, Frances and her family, or the talk I had with Emily about womanly matters, seemed trivial now. Mama seemed very concerned about sending packages of clothing and envelopes of money to relatives in Poland. Tata felt it was a useless gesture. Surely everything she sent would be confiscated by the enemy. 'That dirty sonofobitch Hitler.' Tata often proclaimed in his best broken English and swearing. But he finally relented to Mama sending packages of clothing. By 1940, when Roosevelt was reelected President and the war in Europe escalated full force, Mama decided to continue only in writing letters and adding a few dollars in there..

My repose from all this madness around me went into listening to the radio, reading and concentrating on a decent education. And just as many other Americans at this time, I was in love with movies. Gone With the Wind and The Wizard of Oz would forever stay my favorites.

Christmas Eve of '39 and '40 were quite subdued. Now Tata was looking forward to the new year of 1941 and the war ending soon. I was looking forward to spring, warmer weather, and green trees to walk beneath. Just before spring came, a strange restlessness began to stir inside me. Almost twelve years old, I knew my body was changing. That great change from child to young woman came the same week little Mary died.

Mary grew quite ill about the middle of winter. Although Francis tended to her diligently day and night, this mother's love could not keep death away. Mary died about the time the sweet scent of spring filled the air. Those morning when the air is faintly crisp and that familiar smell of spring freshness mingles dew.. When I walked to school on that day and saw that wreath of white flowers trimmed in white satin ribbon that designated a childs death hanging on the front door of Frances' flat, my heart sank.

I knew Anna would not be attending school on this day, and I wished I could also turn around and return home in my now mournful state. But I did not want to upset Mama, and so continued on with my class that day. The following day, which was Saturday, I finally told Mama what had happened. She hugged me and urged me to visit with the family and deceased child. Families often chose to intern a deceased family member in their home, just as Frances did with her little Mary. Just about anyone could step inside this home for viewing; some from friendship, others out of curiosity. I was filled with both feelings as I entered the living room where Mary's casket sat in the far corner of the room.

The pungent smell of sweet flowers filled the room. One could not help but notice immediately the white coffin draped with a canopy of white lace. Surrounded by numerous bouquets tied with white satin ribbon, many people were kneeling in fervent prayer beside the white and silver casket that held the little girl.

I stepped closer. Finding my way around the kneeling bodies, I reached the casket and looked inside. How angelic she looked in her white lace dress; her little fingers holding a tiny rosary. I felt so forlorn at seeing this tiny girl laying here. When I heard the quiet sobbing of Mary's mother and father, aunt and grandparents, my sadness grew so profound I could hardly keep from turning and running out the door. I was remembering another wake and another angelic face, but that never stirred the mixed feelings of anger and bewilderment that this one did. Why would God want to take this child from a family who loved her so much? That, only one of the questions I asked myself as I lay in bed that evening. My safe world was changing too much...too quickly. As was my young innocent body. Two days later I went to Mama and told her I awakened with blood on my pajamas. She smiled and hugged me and asked me if I read the little booklet she gave me explaining this change in my body. I told her I did, and I knew what to expect every month now. I never mentioned my enlightening talk with Emily.

I embraced summer vacation this year with open arms. I was a bit embarrassed at how quickly my body was beginning to bloom now. I was never so glad to have summer vacation arrive and relieve me of all those gawking boys. This summer I not only had Rosemary to chum around with, but also planned on visiting with Alice and Frances as well. Frances was now rather quiet and subdued, no doubt still grieving her loss. Alice tried to cheer her up as we sat on the front steps talking about their new neighbor. If anyone could drive the blues away, it would be someone like Ziggy.

Patrick Flannery, unshaven, his wild blond hair flying in the wind as he zig-zagged from street to street on his motorcycle, thus the nickname 'Ziggy'. Always dressed in a white T-shirt, black trousers and black boots, Ziggy never took life too seriously. Always joking, forever flirting with Alice, he was handsome in a rough sort of way. His only joy came from working on his bike, a few cars in the neighborhood and zooming around on his bike. By the end of summer we would find out what we saw outside was not what Ziggy was inside. Just before school started again in September, Ziggy vanished...so it seemed. Alice told me he decided to enlist in the army. I longed to see him in his uniform. Surely he must have looked different. That chance never came, for Ziggy never returned home. Perhaps Frances had been right in her observation of Ziggy. He was a free spirit who needed flight. A year after he enlisted Ziggy was killed in battle. If one believes in reincarnation, Ziggy surely came back as a bird.

As much as I disliked all that had happened since 1939, 1940 did also bring many wonderful new industries: a drive-in restaurant named McDonalds and a new candy called M & M. Unemployment fell in 1940, due to increasing factory orders spurred by the war. Now, as we looked forward to 1941, Tata hoped things might get better yet. I told him once I just wished everything could stay the same, just as his tree. He smiled and said I was wrong about his tree…that too changed just as much as the world around us. Just as our world changed with the times, so too did his tree with the changing seasons. So little by little, I began to understand and perhaps even accept that changes had to come…they were inevitable.

Just as my body had changed, and was still changing, so did my feelings toward boys. When Earl McLean started Hamline School in fall of 1940, I thought I had died and gone to heaven. Never had I seen such beautiful black hair and blue eyes. His smile stirred feelings in my stomach that both frightened and exhilarated me. I had my first taste of falling in love. Unfortunately Earl was just as shy as I was. The most that came from my unrequited love was one or two conversations during recess, and smiles across the room. Hardly a story-book romance. So I looked to more exciting things.

Our first introduction to sliced white bread was a good consolation prize for the loss of my first love. Wrapped neatly in its own colorful paper, I looked upon this delight as yet another change in the progress of life. But this new concept of white bread brought about consequences far greater then I might have imagined.

Silvercup Baking Company was situated on Garfield Boulevard. One could not miss this tall building that sat in an area once considered plush with its large brick homes. It was inevitable we pass Silvercup at least twice a month, during any one of our excursions to Jackson Park. To the beach, to the museum, or for a stroll through a place we named 'the circle', we now began to notice something else during those Sunday morning drives toward our Sunday adventure. The wonderful scent of baking bread engulfed our senses on those mornings. I knew the bakers were busy baking bread and sweet rolls for Monday distribution to grocery stores. The smell wafted into the rolled down windows of Tata's car like a bee ready to sting me with its existence. My nostrils quivered at this very familiar scent from ovens filled with delectable food. Even I, who recognized this smell, inhaled its deliciousness. What delight, I thought, the families in this neighborhood experienced now as this unfamiliar scent reached their nose. Surely, just as mine, their mouth watered in anxiousness to taste this new form of white bread.

At the beginning Mama's mind was fixed on not purchasing Silvercup Bread. 'Not as good as Tata's bread.' She reminded me, or: 'what an insult to his baking should we dare to try this new bread.' Eventually, we did dare. Mama was just as curious as anyone else. So in due time, but with explicit directions that Tata not know about it, she sent me across the street to the little grocery store and in great secrecy I purchased a loaf of the soft white bread.

Soft and spongy. That is how Mama described this bread upon first taste. She compared it to the crusty, solid white bread sold in our bakery and I felt sure that would be the end of any more Silvercup bread. Surprisingly, Mama began using it for sandwiches and for toast, confessing that it was not quite as dry as the other bread. One loaf usually lasted two weeks. Soon it became more difficult to hide our secret delight from Tata. It was on a day Mama, Halina and I were out shopping that Tata found a half eaten loaf tucked away in our pantry. Mama thought she had hidden it well behind cans of fruit and soup. Mama had also taken to buying cans of soup whenever all her homemade soup was gone. Tata was looking to open a can of that soup, and found the bread. When we returned home from shopping, Tata was sitting at the kitchen table enjoying a bowl of soup and a slice of our white bread and butter.

Tata never said a word, nor did Mama. Years later, in recounting this story, Mama said she should have remembered how willing Tata always was to try new food…how open he always was to changes. Ironically, Silvercup Baking Company would one day be his last place of employment before retiring. What drove him to that building on Garfield was a much bigger force then Silvercup Baking Company. One that would bring many people to their knees, in a manner of speaking, or better still, to a new way of shopping. It was called a supermarket…the The Atlantic and Pacific, or A & P, the first to open its doors in the Back of the Yards area.

When this progressive market opened its large store on 47th Street, it changed and surely excited the course of grocery shopping. And very quickly, the little grocery store just around the corner, became extinct. The first time I went shopping with Mama at A&P, I could see why this new store with rows of shelving that stacked a variety of food might excite the shopper. Strolling down each isle was as pleasant as walking through the park. Mama tried to stay true to the grocer where she bought most of her staples. But the pleasurable feast of so many different choices at the large market soon took hold. A feast that hurt Tata as well.

This new supermarket was based on packaged goods. One of the companies contributing packaged bread and sweet rolls was Silvercup. Wrapped bread, buns and sweet rolls was a unique trend in bakery goods. Not only did the housewife purchase bread neatly wrapped, the bread stored easily and stayed fresh in its own wrapping. Little by little, as customers frequented the supermarket, the small grocer had to cut down on his stock. Which also meant less deliveries for Tata. Which diminished his income.

I have no doubt Tata and Mama discussed this dilemma to great lengths. Halina and I never heard any of these conversation. My parents felt we were too young to partake in such discussions, and certainly too young to help decide any alternatives. Yet although we were sheltered from such problems, I could not help but notice that Tata's deliveries were less and less each day. The news that our bakery would be

149

closing came just as autumn was coming to an end in 1940. Joe, our precinct captain was visiting with Tata that day. I noted the somber look on Tata's face as he stood at the kitchen door, shaking hands with him and thanking him for helping him find a job at Silvercup. Joe conversed with Tata in Polish, which I understood quite perfectly: 'The neighborhood is going to miss this bakery.' Joe said. 'Progress and change...we cannot stop either one.' Tata answered. Joe put a hand on Tata's shoulder and wished him good luck.

If Mama and Tata chose not to discuss such progress with us, Rosemary and I certainly did. When I told Rosemary our bakery would be closing, it did not surprise her. Slatky's store was not faring any better. 'I look to it closing down soon too.' Rosemary said. Surprisingly it lasted longer then others. Perhaps because of the penny candy, nickel ice cream cones, and a place to sit on the steps eating both. The new supermarket would never offer that.

Tata as always was determined not to allow the march of progress to stomp all over him. He was open to new ideas. All he had to do was find a way to take advantage of this new beginning and turn it around to benefit his family and himself. His first step had been to find that new job. He would work the three to eleven shift. Since the forty hour work schedule was adopted nationwide in 1940, his hours were perfect. His second step to new beginnings was to refurbish the entire front of the bakery and turn it into two flats.

The following spring, while many other homes were getting their usual repainting and repair, the entire front of our home was being torn apart. By summers end of '41 the drastic change was complete.

Gone were the two front nooks where Babsha and I once sat looking out unto a cobble stone street and its lazy traffic. That cubby hole where I played with cutout dolls and learned to draw pictures as I watched venders sell their wares, totally gone.

Gone, the showcases that held Tata's scrumptious cakes and marvelous crusty bread. No more shoppers to chat with Mama in wee morning hours as they picked out their breakfast bismarks and after dinner coffee cakes.

Gone, the little kitchen that held Tata's rocker, in which he lulled me to sleep and sang Polish lullabies. The small cot where Tata napped; the table and chairs where he sat decorating Easter lambs or dipped slices of orange in sugar to satisfy my sweet tooth, all gone now.

Tata had little trouble selling the long table that Babsha once used for preparing chicken for Sunday dinner, or her delectable stuffing for Polish sausage. Where Mama and Tata left their colorful New Year Eves hats and noise makers for Halina and me to enjoy New Years Day morning. All a memory now.

Forever I would remember the large square butcher block table Tata used for pounding dough into bread and buns. Brick by brick the massive oven that turned that dough golden brown disappeared. Everything from the front door to the back door of our bakery was sold or torn down and rebuilt. Where once stood Kalinowski's Bakery, there were now two separate flats.

Each flat had two bedrooms, living room, bathroom and kitchen. The front flat, a front entrance and one from the gangway. The back flat also had one entrance from the side, plus another off the porch. The entrance to our basement, once in the small kitchen now existed from the gangway. By the end of that summer Tata also converted the hissing coal furnace into oil heating. No more coal delivery; no more ashes to carry out. The only time Tata or Mama needed to unlatch that little door was to pull out the hose for watering down the sidewalk, gutter, and nurturing Tata's tree. That at least stayed the same...the sweeping, the watering...like clock work. This task remained a faithful continuity in my ever changing world. His tree stood tall and unwavering to change.

By fall Tata was well imbedded into his forty hour week at Silvercup. Those of us who ignored the European war, now felt the effect of the first peacetime draft conducted in the United States. More couples began to get married...either to avoid the draft or have someone home waiting for their return. Stella's son, Bill, was drafted, as was a Koczubowski boy. By fall our two flats were rented. Mr. and Mrs. Claveau and their family of three girls lived in the front flat. A newly married couple, Mr. and Mrs. Flannigan, in the back flat.

Mrs. Claveau was short in stature and claimed Irish heritage. Her orange-red hair and eyes as pale blue as the morning sky confirmed her claim. She was prone to a protruding round belly, which no doubt came from the good food she cooked and ate and the beer she and Mr. Claveau enjoyed every evening. Mr. Claveau was French by heritage. He considered himself a Frenchman in name only. A fourth generation American, he hated when anyone asked him what his nationality was. Tall and lanky, he was full of boundless energy. He not only helped Mama sweep and water the sidewalk every week-end, he also scrubbed the floors and washed the windows for Mrs. Claveau. He was just as effervescent in playing with his three small daughters.

Mr. and Mrs. Flannigan were quiet. I hardly ever saw them. Mrs. Flannigan always brought the monthly rent to our door, until one month, when it was late and Mama had to go downstairs and knock on their door. That morning, as we sat around the table eating supper, Mama mentioned to Tata that she was not happy at the way the Flannigan's flat looked. Apparently Mrs. Flannigan was not the best of housekeepers. Mama said she hated to say anything to Mrs. Flannigan. Tata insisted she had to. 'It is still our home', Tata explained. Though the Flannigans were paying rent, both flats had to be cared for by the tenants living there. I was sitting on the porch, enjoying a bit of winter sunshine and reading a book when Mama knocked on Mrs. Flannigan's door. Mama asked Mrs. Flannigan if she could step inside for a moment. I do not know what was discussed, but that week-end Mr. Flannigan washed their living room windows and Mrs. Flannigan eventually began scrubbing the porch floor at least once a month.

Winter was creeping in quickly. Walking to the library beneath the trees of red and gold leaves, the air crisp and alive, I was looking forward to what would be my final year in grammar school. This Christmas we would probably enjoy the company of Mrs. Gongolova, Mr. Chmielewski and Teddy, and Mr. and Mrs. Karczewski, old friends from the Polish choir who traveled quite extensively in previous years and were finally settled this year.

My eight grade class would be the last one graduating in January. Hamline no longer had A & B classes. September would now be the beginning of every school year and June for graduation. My class would fare the same in high school, being the last to graduate in January.

My hair was past shoulder length now, Rosemary's finally grown back to almost her shoulders. Overalls were long gone from my wardrobe…slacks in the winter, shorts in the summer. Years seemed to be passing so swiftly now…'39, '40, and now '41 almost gone. My love for handsome Earl vanished as quickly as it started. In eight grade I discovered Earl had much higher aspirations then falling in love. Rosemary convinced me of this. 'Look at him, always sitting by himself.' Rosemary remarked one day at recess. 'Because he's shy. I talked to him a few times. He seems like a very shy nice boy.' I defended the once love-of-my-life. 'Well, yesterday Alvin tried talking to him and Earl told him to bug off.' Rosemary said. I could hardly believe anyone could be rude to Alvin. He was really a shy little boy. Short for his age, the thick rimmed glasses he wore seemed too big for his small face. His clothing, although raggedy, was clean, but hung rather restlessly on Alvin's thin body. Well, I would just find out why Earl rebuffed Alvin. After all, Earl did talk to me.

My stomach did its still usual flip-flop as I sauntered over to where Earl sat…on the ground, his back resting against the high metal fence. He seemed engrossed in a book.

'How are you today?' I asked casually. 'Fine.' He answered without looking up.

'Are you O.K.?' Now he looked up at me. 'Sure.' He answered. 'Why do you ask?'

'Because you hurt little Alvins feeling by telling him to bug off.'

'Look.' Earl put his book down and looked up at me. 'I really don't want to get involved with friends. I plan on attending college after I graduate from high school. I don't have time for childish games.' And went back to reading.

I was disappointed in what I once thought so perfect. I walked back to where Rosemary stood watching me. 'You're right. He is too absorbed in other plans. No time for us.' I dare not tell her what I really felt was terribly stupid for having loved Earl once.

December came with promises of my very first lipstick and a small container of Coty's face powder that Christmas Eve. I felt fantastically feminine and felt confident there were 'other' Earls in the world ready to be conquered.

I, who had laughed at Emily land Alice and their romanticism, was slowly falling into the same trap. One I did not see. One I certainly enjoyed searching for. I was lured into this trap quietly. With passionate romantic stories, in books, on the radio…all giving me a clue to where my thoughts and desires were heading. Clues I hardly paid much heed to.

The passion I had for listening to the radio swept over me like a lovers touch: The Lux Theatre, The Shadow, Woman in White and Young Dr. Malone; and on the lighter side, The Quiz Kids and Red Skelton. Books such as Tender is the Night or For whom the Bell Tolls, further motivated my romantic thoughts. But the music, beautiful romantic music of the forties, it etched my mind with such colorful and fervent dreams. I felt like a butterfly discovering a remarkable garden of flowers as my mind soared from song to song: I'll Never Smile Again, Careless, Imagination, Fools Rush In, I hear a Rhapsody, Tonight We love and Intermezzo. Any extra money I had now went for sheet music and movies. Extra hours were filled with reading and listening to the radio.

Rosemary and I noticed how congested downtown was becoming. The automobile drastically altered internal circulation. There was talk of building a superhighway and subway to radiate this traffic away from the Loop. Still, we enjoyed our walks through the Loop and the beautifully Christmas decorated windows.

Mama was feeling a bit better this winter season. So much so that she was working part time at A & P tomato packing factory. She told us about the troop trains that came by the factory on the way to boot camp. She also promised me I could work with her at this factory the following year, when I turned fourteen. And Alice, who was so fearful of becoming an old maid, was getting married to a career Army man. By the end of December she would be living in Texas with her new husband.

The world around me still seemed relatively safe and sound at the beginning of December, 1941. But soon, the potpourri of service men that already roamed Chicago's Loop would increase…as would the troop trains. My world, as every one elses, was about to change and never be the same again.

HIGH SCHOOL AND WORLD WAR II

I had three things on my mind at the beginning of this December in 1941: graduation, high school and putting money aside for Christmas presents. On December 7th, Halina and I were enjoying an afternoon movie at Peoples Theatre. Afterwards I urged her to hurry home so we wouldn't miss one of our favorite afternoon broadcasts, The Shadow. Evenings were wonderful for the best of the best broadcasts…Grand Central Station always had marvelous stories and Inner Sanctum sent chills through my spine from beginning to end. But on Sunday, it was The Shadow. We reached the kitchen door about ten minutes before it began with the Shadows deep eerie laugh. We said a quick 'Hello' to Mama and Tata. They were sitting at the kitchen table drinking coffee and eating a slice of pound cake. We hurried toward the back bedroom as we pulled of jacket, cap, and gloves. They would have to wait for proper placement after the Shadow gave his last deep laugh and said 'The Shadow knows.' I threw my belongings on the small sofa next to the radio and plopped myself down for an afternoon of relaxation.

The voice I heard after turning on the radio sounded familiar. Although I understood perfectly well most of what President Roosevelt was saying, I had to look up the new word I heard in his speech: 'infamy' This day, according to him, was a day of infamy. Notoriously evil; shamefully bad; wicked…this is how the dictionary described that word, this day and what it meant. Without warning, with evil intent, Japan had attacked Pearl Harbor. Americans were killed; battleships sunk. Japan also attacked the Philippines, Wake Island and Guam. On the following day, the United States declared war on Japan.

I ran back into the kitchen with this horrible news. Tata shook his head. 'So, another demon from Hell has now invaded our country as well. They are one—the devil in Europe and the one in Japan. We must be ready for many changes. The struggle to regain peace will be great.'

Peace did not come easily. By December eleventh Germany and Italy declared war on the United States. Blackouts and air raid tests soon took the place of peaceful evenings not only on Loomis, the entire country as well.

War has a way of unearthing not only our spirituality but other emotions and passions as well. Courage and strength were undeniable traits early immigrants brought to this country. It showed again during the great depression. Now their sons and daughters would show the same fortitude in the face of adversity.

Our Eve was a solemn celebration in 1941. Church attendance doubled this year. As Mama promised, I began working part time at A & P's tomato factory shortly after the new year began. Working with Mama and all the other women, only a few as young as myself, we talked and laughed and shared our lives during these working hours. I worked a couple of hours after school, eight hours on Saturday. Mama continued working about six hours a day, which really put a kink in her schedule. Her Monday wash was done in the evening, as was the ironing. I helped with the housework every Friday, having most of it complete before she came home from work.

The tomato factory faced the railroad tracks on one side. Originally placed here for shipment of all the vegetables packed here and shipped to other cities. The windows in the room where we packaged tomatoes faced those tracks, and almost every Saturday we could count on a troop train filled with young men going off to camp roll pass the windows. The train rolled by slowly at this point, many times stopping, probably to switch tracks. All of the young women, and a few of the older ones, would stop their packing and run to the windows...waving eagerly to the smiling faces on that train. Some trains carried young men just enlisted, others carried men in uniform...perhaps enroute to a point where they would ship out. Regardless, they seemed just as eager to wave back at us. My part time job lasted all summer and ended just before graduation. Because of so many men being drafted or enlisting, only women who could work four hours a day or more were being hired.

Rubber rationing began at the end of December in '41. That winter I was proudly wearing a ribbon of blue and gold ribbon that signified my soon to be graduation. My cousin Eddie enlisted in the army and Herby said he could hardly wait until he graduated from high school to join the navy, Aunt Isabelle wrote to Mama.

Tata was well immersed in his three to eleven shift at Silvercup. With his wages, Mama's part time job and rent coming from two flats, I felt very lucky indeed that I was allowed to keep my wages from A & P for personal and school needs. I bought my own graduation dress, shoes and hose with that money.

Butterflies infested my stomach that day in January as I marched down the aisle with my class on this last day in Hamline School. Within one week the change from upper class student in elementary school to lowly freshman at Gage Park High School would come as swiftly as the changes in our neighborhood. Elaine was married to her soldier; all the Wishniewski boys were in the army, as was the Koczubowski clan. We didn't hear the resounding sound of Polkas on Saturday nights any more. When Mama and I attended Sunday Mass at St. John of God, our prayers were for the boys in the service and for a quick end to the war. I felt the solemnity of the times during my graduation as well. The songs we sang were those World war I songs Miss Metzger inspired us to learn. Added now were new songs, from a new war: There'll Be Bluebirds Over the White Cliffs of Dover was added to My Buddy. As Miss Metzger conducted and our final song, When You Wish Upon A Star, I felt sure all the songs meant something different to everyone in that auditorium. I could hear sniffing and blowing of noses. Tears filled many eyes on that stage as well. The songs were a memorial to my days at Hamline and a heralding of new beginnings. To everyone, the words and music surely gave somber knowledge to a questionable future, yet one we dare not doubt or lose faith in.

When I was five years old, Tata and Mama took me to the Chicago Worlds Fair, held in 1933. I was not as awe-struck by these sights as I was on that first day at Gage Park High School. For eight years I walked through a neighborhood familiar with homes and faces and entered a building with dimly lit halls and creaking wood floors. Ninety-nine percent of my classmates came from immigrant parents. We had all been blessed with caring, conscientious teachers who gave us the same teachings of respect and morality taught to us by our parents. All of these years gave us a sturdy foundation to exploring higher expectations from ourselves. In high school, some of these things changed.

Neither Mama nor Tata were the sort of parents to insist I take 'this' or 'that' course. Nor did they have lofty designs on my future. They did insist, and expect, as they had during my eight years of elementary school, that, short of a severe illness, I attend school each day and do my very best at whatever I chose to become after twelve years of schooling. Unfortunately, they never suggested, encouraged, and probably never gave much if any thought, that I go on to higher learning after high school graduation.

In grammar school my grades were average, with one or two above. In high school the challenge would be greater. When Rosemary and I boarded that trolley on 51st and Loomis that first day, we were excited. Transferring to a trolley on Western Avenue that took us to a corner just four blocks shy of Gage Park High School, we had high expectations as we walked toward our new school. What exactly did we expect of our new teachers, our new classmates, and most of all what we planned for our future?

Before I even entered that large three story building on that very first day, the cultural difference from where I lived and those former classmates at Hamline, felt so palpable I had a sudden desire to turn around, go back home and lock myself away in my own little world. Hardly an acceptable choice. I was putting myself down, and it went against the grain of everything and every word instilled in me from birth. 'Never put yourself beneath anyone else...nor be so lofty to put yourself above others' I had to find the courage to live in this strange and new environment for the next four years. 'The fall,' Tata once said, 'hurts more then the climb'. So keeping this in mind, I walked into this building among students who were dressed more fashionably and expensively then I; those who chatted in obvious accent-free English and who seemed much more at home then I did at this moment. And although I found the strength to continue this new journey, my shyness reemerged very quickly. For now I felt new friendships would be few and far between during my high school years.

Too often worries and trepidation are a figment of our own imaginings. I worried about making friends when I started first grade; I worried people would notice a great difference in my appearance when I became a woman…so to speak, at age twelve. Especially since Mama found it difficult to explain the change taking place in my body. Thank goodness for that little book Kotex offered shy mothers and questioning curious daughters. If only I was more like Tata, who always seemed open minded to change. 'If changes never took place,' he reminded me once, 'the world would grow stale. Although some changes are sad, they all come for the same reason—because ideas change and people change.' So I tried to remember this as I began my freshman year. And to my surprise and delight, found this first year an extension of eight grade.

The addition of Home Economics seemed the only difference in an otherwise bland first year of high school. If I attended any football games or class dances, it was only in the hope of familiarizing myself with this new outside world. At the end of each day, and those extracurricular activities, I was so happy…so relieved…even grateful, to get home to my home on Loomis Street. To sit in that secluded bedroom with Halina and listen to our radio; to sit outdoors on our green bench, beneath Tata's sturdy full maple tree—it was here I could really dream of my future. Here the tension of that first spring of my freshman year finally vanished into another summer vacation. But quickly, autumn came again and the remainder of that agonizing year was finally in its last chapter. As December rolled around again, I began to feel on an equal rung with everyone else in my class.

Home Economics not only introduced me to baking brownies, I also met some of those very same students I once thought far removed from my world. They laughed as I did; dreamed as I did, and were as much frightened of the future as anyone else. A few of the girls in my class were in a close

161

relationship with upper class students they knew from grammar school. Their greatest fear that their boyfriends would be drafted or enlist after graduation. A fear not far-fetched, for most young men between 1941 and 1945 did exactly that. As I listened to their concerns and hopes I felt grateful my only worry at this time was what I hoped to do after graduating from high school.

Toward the end of winter in '42 I began a new after school job. A laundry on the west side of Chicago was looking for part time help. Three hours a day after school and four hours on Saturday was perfect for me. Those winter days of bundling up so many times during the day was enough to bring more exhaustion then working after school. Wearing slacks in school was an absolute no-no. During Chicago's sever cold weather, slacks were the only saviour to keeping my legs from becoming pink with frost bite. So they went on, each morning, under a wool skirt. Once in school, they came off as I stood next to my locker. Boots, slacks, plus everything else that necessitated keeping warm, was so time consuming, I rose at least an hour earlier during winter mornings, and departed for school a half hour earlier. If nothing else, it did teach me how to plan my time with punctuality.

Working in the laundry shop taught me the rudiments of properly ironing a starched white shirt, and folding it afterwards for packaging. I promptly displayed my talent to Mama, which delighted her. Tata however, was not about to forsake the Chinese laundry. My laundry shop also introduced me further to a war still so distant to me.

The owners daughter was married to a man who volunteered his pilot abilities by enlisting in the Royal Air Force in England. Shortly after I started working there, the young husband was reported missing in action. Several days later the young wife received a telegram confirming his death. The laundry closed its doors for a two week period. After it opened again, one of the other workers told me the family had much to arrange while they waited for the young man's remains to arrive for burial.

Seeing and hearing all of this...the troops in route, the pilot losing his life, my friends in fear of what the future held for the boys they loved, the world around me seemed spinning out of control. Chicago's Loop was already filled with a potpourri of service men. The thought of a quick end to the war now remained only a that. 1942 brought sugar and gas rationing. Mama and Tata, who seldom talked about the bakery that once was, remarked once it was a blessing they did what they did. Tata had more free time to spend with Mama and more time to visit with Mr. Chmielewski. They both enjoyed mushroom hunting and visiting one another...until that day Mr. Chmielewski was rushed to the hospital to have some gallstones removed. After that, his health deteriorated quickly. Now, with gas rationing, and Tata seldom driving anywhere, he and Mama began to enjoy evenings together, playing cards...Five Hundred Rummy always their best stand-by card game. Tata did miss the game of checkers with his old buddy, who was as home bound as Tata now. For those few times Tata enticed me into a game of checkers, I gladly accepted the challenge. And always lost the game.

Aunt Isabelle and Uncle George were talking about returning to Chicago. Herby would be graduating from high school soon and true to his dreams, he joined the Navy. Mama was still working part time at A & P, packing tomatoes. By 1943 I was ready for other work besides ironing and folding shirts. I quit my job at the laundry and found a part time position at Meyer Brother Department Store on Ashland, in their lay-away department. My job was to make out lay-away slips for customers and also pass out free light bulbs to those who paid their electric bill at this store and brought their burned out bulbs here.

It was a nice change from the steamy laundry, and also closer to home. But when I had to work late that Christmas Eve, because of late shoppers taking out their lay aways on the eve, I learned the same lesson Tata knew when he closed his bakery: the world does not always flow in that direction we might wish it to. As I walked home on this dark Christmas Eve, on sidewalks shiny and slick from freezing wet snow, the Christmas trees inside every cozy looking, twinkling bright, all I could think about was how much I missed being at home with my family. I vowed never to feel this way again. My family, be it the one I

163

had now, or one I might have in the future, would always be together at Christmas time. Fate or God, I had yet to learn, more often then not paid little heed to our vows and dreams and those promises we make to ourselves. As I learned through time, our plans were much easier to erase when others were set in stone.

It is said that time goes quickly when you're having fun. When I began my second year in high school that January of '43, I could say it was only the experience of this newness in my life that made that first year fly by as quickly as the clouds I often watched while sitting on our bench. An experience of two unsuccessful dates also came this year.

Angelo and Jeff both attended Gage Park. Angelo came from that part of our neighborhood near Ashland Avenue that housed a small community of Mexican immigrants. Jeff was from a now occupied Irish community. Angelo was tall and dark and one year older then me. Mama reluctantly allowed me to take a late walk with him one Friday evening. She felt I was too young for evening dating.

Although Angelo was older, he was in the same grade as I was. He was held back a year when he could not grasp the English language as well as was expected. His attitude about this seemed quite rebellious, telling me he did not care if he graduated or not. That as soon as he was old enough, he would enlist. In my romantic youth, I found this rebellion rather fascinating. Besides that, he was very good looking, in a dark mysterious way. Before I went out for that Friday evening walk with Angelo, Mama reminded me again to be very careful. I was fifteen years old, and since my twelfth year, she surely knew my hormones were acting overtime. Which meant I was now aware of the opposite sex. Especially Angelo and his dark handsome ancestry, which stirred me when he held my hand that evening. The strange heavy feeling in my legs and tingling in my stomach came more intensely then with Earl..

'Be careful what you agree to when you go out with a boy.' Mama always warned. Through all my reading, and my talks with Emily, I had some inkling, from an early age, on how babies were made. When my time of maturity arrived, the fear of becoming pregnant dare I go 'too far' with a boy was deeply engrained. To ruin my life, or worse, shame my family, was unthinkable. In many families, unforgivable. So that, when Angelo suggested a walk through Sherman Park that Friday evening, I knew what he was after. My 'girl' talks with Rosemary and Emily and Elaine were often about the girls who gave themselves so easily while laying on the grass with their boyfriends. When I refused Angelo that walk through the park he grew quite angry. 'All I want to do is love you a little bit more…I thought you cared about me?' His words and behavior turned the tingling in my stomach to fear. I remained adamant in my decision. He grew angrier. 'Just take me home.' I finally said. We were only a block away from my home. 'Go ahead, you big baby…walk home yourself. And grow up.' I knew he meant to shame me with those words. But as I walked home I felt rather proud of myself. I never told Mama what happened. She never asked. I related everything to Rosemary—in full detail.

'You were so lucky. Didn't you know about his reputation when he asked you out?'

'No.' I answered. Rosemary went on to tell me Angelo spent many Fridays at Sherman Park, with many different girls. One who no longer attended Gage Park because of pregnancy. Whether or not this was true I still felt grateful for my escape from such a fate. Sadly, after that experience, the green grass and quiet charm of Sherman Park never looked the same to me for a long time after.

Jeff was a quiet boy and quite different from Angelo. He reminded me of Earl…that first love of my life. Dark hair, blue eyes, and a dimpled smile. Mama allowed me an afternoon at the movies with Jeff. I was glad she insisted on this, since I was not prepared for another moonlit walk. If Angelo exude an animal charisma that attracted me to him, Jeff left me stone cold with his lack of civility and childish behavior.

I had high hopes, that Sunday afternoon as Jeff and I walked to Peoples Show for our afternoon movie date. He held my hand, and even stopped to let me browse in the shop windows on Ashland Avenue. Bought our tickets and escorted me very politely down the aisle to our seats. Everything was going quite well. Then the lights went down and the movie started and Jeff pulled out a pack of gum from his shirt pocket. Without offering me as much as a half stick of gum, he began unwrapping each stick and plopping them in his mouth. I felt, well, a bit nauseated by his performance. During the entire movie he talked to me, or tried, with that large wad of gum in his mouth, spittle running down the sides. I could not imagine what his reasoning was for this disgusting display, but by the time the movie ended, my stomach felt a bit queasy. I was just as glad to get home as I had been after that stroll with Angelo. Jeff tried to kiss me good-by that afternoon. Of course I had no desire to place my lips against his. I shook hands with him and thanked him for a lovely afternoon. When I said good-by to him, I really meant it.

So my sophomore year stayed with doubts of meeting the right 'man' in this high school environment. Eddie was certainly more mature, but I knew any dreams of winning his heart were useless. He often spoke of how his mother hoped he might become a priest. I knew I could not compete with that. Although Clement was sweet, I always thought of him more as a brother then a boyfriend. Besides, the service men I viewed each time Rosemary and I went downtown looked so much more manly then the 'boys' in school. Sadly, those week end visits downtown came to an abrupt end when Rosemary met and fell head over heels in love with a Senior. Her new relationship put a damper on our friendship. Except for riding together to and from school, we hardly saw each other any more. And I began to wonder what was wrong with me to have such poor luck in finding someone nice to date. My looks were, to say the least, passable. No, I was not tall and willowy as Rosemary, so perhaps that was it. I felt sure it was, until I met Suzie Vojtek. She dispelled any notions that one had to be slim and tall to attract men.

Suzie began riding the trolley with me in January of '43. She and her family moved into our neighborhood a week before our sophomore year began. Suzie lived in a two story flat just one block from where we caught the trolley. She was beginning her Junior year the morning I met her. Rosemary was home with the flu that day. When Suzie saw me standing alone, without anyone to talk to, she approached me without reservation or shyness. This bulky looking girl, who weighed at least forty pounds more

166

then I did, had very little feminine charm. With her over-permed kinky hair that looked as though it needed a good washing from the oil at its roots, Suzie came off as an out-going, very confident person who was totally unaware of her—ah—defects. From that first day I admired her. She was always friendly. Her conversation so prolific and colorful, I hardly had a chance to get a word in edge wise on that first day. My astonishment did not end with this morning meeting.

Suzie's unusual charm apparently attracted more then just me. That day after school we rode the trolley back home together. When we reached our destination, a young man was waiting for Suzie as we stepped off the trolley. Suzie's boyfriend, to be exact. Tall, blond and quite handsome, he displayed unbiased affection for Suzie. Hugging her, kissing her cheek, taking her books as Suzie turned to me and introduced me to Charlie. 'He's home on leave this week. When I graduate we plan to get married.' Suzie added happily. From the grin on Charlie's face, I could see he agreed with her happiness. As they walked off, Charlie's arm around Suzie's thick shoulders, they looked absolutely blissful. I liked Suzie; she had an inner beauty that obstructed all her other faulty traits. Obviously Charlie realized this also. The following day, as we sat on the bus chatting, Suzie told me Charlie was a childhood friend who had always been her 'sort of guardian angel'. 'Whenever the kids called me names or picked on me, Charlie was there to defend me.' Their love, she said with eyes bright as a new silver dollar, came in her freshman year after Charlie enlisted. They realized then their friendship had grown into a strong love for each other. Still, whatever Suzie and Charlie found, my sophomore year held no such promise.

Aunt Isabelle, in a letter to Mama, wrote of how much she missed Chicago and seeing her sister. She also conveyed an intriguing story, which Mama passed on to all of us at the supper table. As Mama flitted from stove to table, filing each of our plates with golomki, known in America as stuffed cabbage leaves, buttered carrots and mashed potatoes, this is the story she told:

Herbie's dream finally came true. In the navy now, he was stationed aboard a battleship, somewhere in the Pacific. 'On one particular night',as Aunt Isabelle wrote in her letter, 'I heard Herbie's voice call out to me.' His voice, she continued in letter, came so clear it awakened my aunt from her sleep. The bedroom was filled with a strange eerie gray smoke. In the center of the bedroom, an image of Herbie appeared...his arms extended to her. 'I rose from my bed immediately and knelt down beside it.' With head bent, Aunt Isabelle prayed fervently to God that He watch over her son. When she raised her head and opened her eyes the smoke and image were gone. A week later Aunt Isabelle received a letter from Herbie. In it he wrote, as much as he could, of an explosion on the battleship and how close he had been to that area of this explosion. By some miracle he was summoned top-side. Numerous men had been injured, some fatally. By the Grace of God, Herbie had been spared.

My aunt always had an innate gift for fortune telling. Mama had no doubt whatsoever that Aunt Isabelle was in some way instrumental in helping save her sons life. I was always mystified how well Aunt Isabelle told my fortune with a mere deck of normal playing cards. I always thought she should have opened her very own fortune telling parlor. Compared to the gypsies on Ashland Avenue, Mama also believed better what her own sister foretold through those cards. Unfortunately, Mama never elaborated if any of the predictions came true.

Rationing continued in America. Shoes and canned goods, meat, cheese and fat were added in February and March. The Polio epidemic was spreading across the United States which prompted Mama to remind us constantly that we wash our hands before putting any food in our mouth.

When spring came it was difficult to realize that a war was raging in Europe and the Pacific, or that we had to be so careful least we contract the dreaded polio. Grass was turning emerald green on every front lawn in the Back of the Yards community. Tata's tree, with its broad green leaves, began to fill with the tranquility of summer time. When April came and Rosemary revealed to me that her sister was getting married and soon they would be moving to a city north of Chicago, I knew another chapter in my life was ending. We promised to write to each other, but I think we both knew how much our togetherness had waned since starting high school. Now, with her moving, I felt certain the pages of our friendship were coming to a close…but never to be forgotten as some of the most cherished memories of my childhood. When my homeroom teacher read her interesting letter from the school board that fresh April morning my senses became filled with more then the smell of lilacs and crisp morning dew. I knew my life was about to change as well.

'In 1944 you will be starting your junior year.' The letter began, 'Jones Commercial High School will be accepting transfers at this time. In attending this school you will not only complete your third and fourth year of high school, but graduate with the assurance that you will have received the finest education in preparation for the business field.' Which more clearly meant, although Jones Commercial was a co-ed school, more transfers would be expected from the young women at Gage Park then young men.

To those who were looking forward to getting married as soon as they graduated from high school, the choice was simple: stay at Gage Park and continue on with Home Economics. For others, myself included, I wanted more from life then baking brownies and cookies and cooking roast beef to tenderness.

'We will offer counseling all summer to help you decide what classes might best suit you, should you decide to transfer. Just fill out this card and we will set up a summer date and time for you session.'

So in January of 1944 I began attending Jones Commercial High School. My session the summer before had gone well, but not without disappointment.

'Journalism? Why would you want to be a journalist?' The male face with jowl cheeks and tight lips asked me. His piercing eyes intimidated me from behind thick glasses.'It sounds interesting.' I answered in a timid voice. And trying to defend my quest, added: 'I often dream of how lovely to be part of such writing skills.'

'It's a mans world, journalism.' Mr. Jaws leaned over the desk to bring his point closer. 'Do you realize how ostracized a woman would be in that world.' His voice sounded very unconvincing in its monotone range. 'Well, I'd like to find out for myself.' I added, hopeful. 'No, I simply do not recommend this for you. Here, this is the perfect course for a woman.' And handed me a card that read: Business Etiquette and Office Machines. 'Don't look so forlorn. With this course you will still get enough English to keep your appetite wet for writing. Perhaps in the future…who knows.'

So there it was. I who had been raised by a family of immigrants who struggled to find independence and freedom of choice, bowed to societies expectations. In retrospect, the word' future' gave me saving grace to continue on. In January of 1944, as I took that first of many street car rides to downtown, and began my last two years of high school in Jones Commercial, a new world beckoned to me.

Darlene Freulich and I hit it off immediately. Her birthday on February 10th, mine on February 9th, we were soul sister Aquarians. She was a first generation born American, both her parents German immigrants. She enjoyed reading, movies and hated any sort of athletic activity. With her upbringing and work ethics much the same as mine, our friendship was a given.

Darlene was a tiny little thing, always spotlessly immaculate in her perfectly ironed dresses, or blouses, well manicured nails and never a hair out of place. She really outdid what I considered perfect. Mrs. Freulich, Darlene's mother, was a charming little lady with hair so white and a body so perfectly round, she reminded me of a female Santa. Darlene's home was located on the west side of Chicago, in a neighborhood that sported larger front and back lawns, and houses spaced further apart then where I lived. Their small cottage sat back behind a front lawn filled with flowers and thick green grass. Mr. Fruelich worked in a steel factory and spoke only a bit more English then Tata. Darlene's parents expected the same thing from her as Mama and Tata did from me: attend school faithfully, get educated and find a good job after you graduate; if you should be so lucky, a nice Polish (German in Darlene's case) man, get married, raise a family.

Darline and I certainly carried out that first request. When I began looking for another part time job that first year at Jones, Darlene joined me in the endeavor. Unfortunately for Darlene, I found the perfect job at Wrigley Brothers Gum Factory, which was close to my home, but too far for her.

The location of Wrigley Gum factory, on 35th and Ashland and my after school work hours, four thirty to nine thirty, were perfect. School hours ended at three thirty at Jones, and the street car I rode home went right by Wrigley's. I went to work right after school, then caught another street car after work, which took me to 49th and Ashland. There would be a dozen or so other women working with me on this shift, all of us part time, and most of us high school students. We worked the belt conveyor that carried unsold pieces of gum. Our job was to pick out those hard pieces and could no longer be reused in processing fresh gum and discard them. The job was remarkably easy...brainless, as I told Darlene after a week of working there. What I enjoyed most was the half hour break we got. Mornings I always wrapped an extra sandwich with me to enjoy during this break. Best of all we had a juke box in the small lounge, which played our favorite songs that helped us reminisce about all the handsome boys in uniform. Most of the girls were going steady with a service man. Those of us who were not as lucky yet could only dream as we listened to our favorite songs.

It was not difficult to feel the romance this decade provided. It was everywhere—the movies: Casablanca; For Me and My Gal; Stage Door Canteen; Spellbound. But it was the music, more then anything, that put butterflies in my stomach...Tonight We Love; There Are such Things; Sleepy Lagoon; You'll Never Know; I'll Be Seeing You; The More I See You—the song titles meant nothing less then love land romance.

I believe my childhood ways ended on my sixteenth birthday. Mama, in her love and trying to please the obvious fancy I now had for service men, especially those in the Navy, decided to throw a sweet sixteen party for me. She invited Emily, Suzie and Darlene. I am sure if Emily and Suzie knew she would also be inviting sailors from Great Lakes Naval Training Center, they may have declined coming to that party.

After all, Suzie was spoken for, her boyfriend overseas now; Emily was just beginning her relationship with the man she would soon marry. But it wasn't as though Mama was trying to be a match maker. She wanted to have a nice party for me and thought I would enjoy the men she chose to invite.

If nothing else, the party opened my eyes to the sadness of this war. All of sailors that came to my party were young and handsome and terribly serious. They were light hearted and gay as we sat at the dining room table enjoying cake and ice cream. Afterwards, when we sat in the living room chatting, the sailors talked about the families, sweethearts, the cities and little towns they left behind and missed terribly. The pride in their voice when they talked about what faced them once they received their orders was unmistakable. Boys who quickly became men as soon as they enlisted, brought a finality to my thinking. It was time to grow up and realize there was more to this world of mine then Loomis Street and The Back of the Yards. A painful realization, to say the least, but one that turned me into an adult that day.

Just as Tata took care of his tree with careful nurturing, I now knew more then ever my future depended on me...no one else. Mama and Tata laid a firm sturdy foundation for my life. The different rooms they built on that foundation would stay with me forever. One room where Mama taught me how to keep a home clean and orderly, yet filled with love. Another room that showed me how to embrace each day with continuity and joy. That special room that taught me to treasure the feminine side of myself. It was not only the application of cream to face and neck, proper clothing and make-up that enhanced a woman's beauty. Tolerance, respect and gentleness towards others meant more then the shade of lipstick one wore. Without the important qualities, all other ingredients were superfluous.

Tata's rooms were built in a cluster of love, hard work and acceptance of our frail human nature. His greatest gift to me was the room that taught me where my roots began, and to work with boldness and tenacity to keep those roots alive. As he watered his tree daily, with so much care, so much devotion and the absolute certainty that his nurturing would help that tree grow strong and sturdy, so too was his dream for me.

By summer and June of '44, my world and the world around me began to look brighter. Tata and Mama, along with the world, were jubilant at hearing and reading about the allied invasion on beaches of Normandy, France. All of us had prayed long and hard for this to come about. This same summer Elaine's husband returned home for good. Clara came home on leave, proudly displaying her WAC uniform and the tall burly soldier boyfriend. The only disappointment this summer was the assassination attempt on Hitler's life that failed.

Eddie entered the service just before Paris was liberated on August 25th. After the army discharged him he came to say good-bye to me and told me he was entering the seminary. I would see him one more time, during the Christmas season of '45. He looked deliriously content and peaceful in his black suit and stiff white collar of a priest.

Darlene and I continued our Saturday evening strolls through Chicago's Loop. Now I felt I had more to offer every serviceman. I became a better listener as they talked about what they had left behind to fight for their country. Since I was still too young to work in the USO canteen, located in downtown Chicago, being a sister of sorts to these service men took the place of passing out do-nuts and coffee and dancing with service men. I met some delightfully charming men during this time. I never met a service man that was disrespectful or vulgar. Our kisses good-night, or in most cases, good-bye, were never about petting or sex. They always conveyed gratitude that I had taken time to be with them while they were away from home and that I listened to their happy and sad tales. I corresponded with many of them afterwards. The letters I received were as poignantly sweet as our conversations and kiss good-bye.

When Roosevelt was reelected for a record fourth term in 1944, I am sure he prayed as much as anyone else the war would end soon. Mr. and Mrs. Claveau moved to the country this summer. Farming looked inviting to Mr. Claveau. I would miss them. Mr. and Mrs. McNulty moved in shortly after. A couple as different from Claveaus as night from day.

Mrs. McNulty, or Betty, as she preferred being called, and her husband Jim, both with dark hair and blue eyes, were as Irish as, as they always said, 'Pattys Pig'. Happy go lucky, they seemed without worry or care. Jim was tall and lanky, Betty short and petite. Their propensity to be so easy going reminded me so much of Tata's personality, which in itself was not a bad trait. For Betty, who had two small children to care for while Jim was off working, this characteristic came close to causing a disaster.

It happened on a summer morning, just as I was walking back through the gangway, after hosing down the sidewalk. Most mornings at this time Betty's children would be sitting at the kitchen table eating breakfast. They were adorable. Jimmie, age six, was the exact replica of his father. Joey was a lovely wide eyed two year old just in the midst of discovering the world around him. Not seeing either at the kitchen table I stopped to peer in the kitchen widow, hoping to catch a glimpse of them. Jimmie was sitting on the floor playing with some little cars, while Joey walked around aimlessly, no doubt in search of something to do. On a pulled out chair, next to the kitchen table, sat a bucket. A bucket I knew Betty used when scrubbing her kitchen floor. I could only hope it was not filled with water as Joey sauntered closer to the bucket. Where was Betty? I asked myself.

As Joey reached up and began to tackle the forbidden fruit I knocked on the kitchen window, hoping to divert his attention. He smiled and waved and continued his task. Within seconds the bucket, filled with water, came tumbling down on him and everything else around him. Betty, who apparently had been on the phone in the living room, came rushing in as soon as she heard the thud. 'Jimmie, why didn't you stop your brother?' She asked the still sitting-still playing smiling boy. When she saw me outside the window, Betty motioned for me to please come in and help. 'What a mess to clean up. Thank the Lord the water was cold. I have been waiting for a phone call before tackling the floor. I guess I don't have to worry about that now'. Betty said as I held Joey in my arms, while Betty mopped the entire kitchen floor. Jimmie casually moved his cars to the porch and with a personality embedded in his genes, continued playing with his toys as though nothing had happened.

Then there was the time Jimmie had to be reprimanded for using his slingshot inappropriately. Big Jim adored his boys. The slingshot he put together for Jimmie was meant only for target practice. That target not being the birds Jimmie decided on one day. Thankfully his aim was terrible. When one of his miscalculated aims with a little stone hit Betty in the arm she finally woke up to what he was trying to do. She was sitting on the bench with Joey, Jimmie behind her, taking full aim at Tata's tree and the two birds perched on a branch. Betty turned around as soon as the stone hit her.

'James Michael McNulty, get over her this instant.' Betty yelled, her anger quite evident. Jimmie came and stood in front of her. Head bowed, sling shot behind him, Betty reached around his body and pulled it away from its hiding place. 'Why don't you just go and play in the traffic Jimmie. That should keep you out of mischief for a long time.' Jimmie looked up at her, his eyes wide with surprise. I was sitting on Kreml's steps reading. Until Betty's suggestion, I almost oblivious to what was going on. By now I was rather used to Jimmies rowdy behavior. Was she serious? I looked up, wondering what might happen next.

Jimmie dropped the slingshot in Betty's lap and began crying.

'Stop it Jimmie. You know I love you. If anything happened to you I would surely die. Now don't you suppose somewhere out there is a mother bird who would feel exactly the same if you killed one of her baby birds? Those little birds have just begun to fly. And here you stand wanting to take that joy away from them.'

By now Jimmie was in full tears. He sat down on the bench and lay his head against Betty's shoulder. 'I'm sorry Mom. I won't do it again.'

Betty tilted her head down against his and said: 'I know you won't. Those are God's creatures son, we have to take care of them. Now here, take your slingshot back and enjoy it properly.'

Betty looked at me, winked and smiled. I smiled back and went back to my reading. Jimmie, I felt sure, was just as relieved as I that the scolding ended. Afterwards, I never saw him aim at Tata's tree, or any other, again.

Witnessing this myriad of marriages...the wonderful one Mama and Tata had, others in our neighborhood, those who seemed devoted to one another, or at the least tolerated one another yet stayed together, and now the different sort of married tenants that occupied our flats, I began to wonder: what would my own marriage be like one day. Yet my thoughts never went any further then only wondering. Despite the few dates I had, none stirred me enough to any serious relationship. Thoughts of a husband and family in my future were rather obliterated by other things. School and studies, an occasional school dance, followed by an occasional evening at the movies. I found both the dance and date rather juvenile after those encounters with service men who were more 'man' then any in school. And working after school hardly gave me time to ponder that much on a future marriage. Homework, reading, writing letters to service men occupied most of my spare time. I wonder now how I managed to find time for week-ends jaunts to the Loop.

If the war brought people together in friendship and prayer, it also tore apart neighborhoods with the disease of bigotry. My own neighborhood, once so completely friendly and bending to differences, suddenly became afflicted with a sudden outbreak of prejudice. Many Poles and Czechs felt that because St. Augustine Church catered primarily to the German populace and presented one Sunday Mass completely in German, they had a conspiracy of sorts with Nazi Germany. Perhaps even hiding German spies inside the hallowed walls of this Franciscan Order. A rumor no doubt started by intolerance and stupidity. Since this church was just around the corner from where we lived, Mama had no qualms about attending Mass at St. Augustine Church. She thought the accusations ludicrous. Tata merely shook his head and said: 'And the same people who start such rumors think nothing of attending mass and receiving Holy Communion every Sunday.' He called such people hypocrites.

Now, for the first time in my life, I witnessed this strong division of thoughts and beliefs that pitted neighbor against neighbor. So it came as no surprise to me when the priest announced one Sunday from his pulpit that St. Augustine would discontinue the early morning mass with German readings. Of course, even after everyone discovered the rumors were false. The damage was done. After the war ended some fingers still stayed pointed at blameless bodies. St. Augustine never resumed the German mass.

I, who had always felt safe and secure behind this invisible fence of open-mindedness, fairness and tolerance, realized how ambiguous these surroundings were. While I still felt safe in my home, or sitting on the green bench with lacy shadows of Tata's tree hovering over me, I now knew the memories and convictions of my childhood would and had to be tested by a world much bigger and different then this one. Now I really missed what I once had. Those days of mushroom hunting with Tata and Mr. Chmielewski; trips to the beauty salon with Mama, the little grocery stores that once dotted our neighborhood, and of course those wonderful unmatched years with Babsha. It seemed I had grown up much too quickly. As beautiful and exciting as my new life was, I often longed to be that little girl again that listened to the morning church bells and walked to St. John of God for her Easter basket blessing.

A new German bakery opened its doors in 51st Street this year. Mama, forever curious, purchased a cheese cake to celebrate Tata's birthday this July 4th. It was the most marvelous cheese cake I had ever tasted. Baked in an oblong pan, with a thin graham cracker crust. Light and fluffy, my taste buds barely getting a chance to enjoy the sweet cheese flavor before melting down my throat like cotton candy. Tata, I could see, gave this cake high points by having two slices with his cup of coffee. Later that evening, as we sat outdoors on our green bench, I asked Tata if he felt any regrets at closing the bakery. We always conversed in Polish. Tata still had not mastered enough English to carry on a full conversation in the language of the country that adopted him. This translation is close to how he answered my question:

'We do not move on because we have to. We move on because it is essential to living a full life. We care for ourselves and our family, we nurture our spirit and our life. And we grow. Sometimes we have to fight very hard and very long to make any change come out right. Tenacity and flexibility is important in any change. We must be very careful not to allow apathy to enter our life. I closed the bakery because it was the right thing to do, for my family. Everything else in my life—my house, my tree, my neighborhood, would mean nothing without my family. Yet I must respect everything. Because for now, everything here is also a part of my life.'

His words were so simple to understand: I know he was telling me that from the very beginning he had to fight for what he believed in. Just as I now understood the passion of this war, what it meant to the men and women who fought it, and the people back home who stood behind them, I had to accept any changes still to come. It was how I faced them and grew with them that was important.

My passion thus far had been that of a child and her memories. The longing for that past. Now I began to feel that stirring in my body and soul that was akin to what Tata felt and wanted as a young man: someone in my life to care for and who would care for me...and a family. Not that family that belongs strictly to a child; my search was now for the grown-up kind. The sweetness of living in a neighborhood where I could raise my own family...perhaps beneath another maple tree with shade in the summer and falling red leaves in autumn.

When Darlene and I took our usual escape to the Loop that one Saturday in August, I half-prayed I might meet someone who might make my dreams come true. I wore my best yellow dress that Saturday. Tata remarked how lovely my shoulder length page-boy looked. Mama reminded me not to stay out too late.

I looked up at the marquee lights as we strolled along State Street. Despite strong feelings that the war in Europe would soon end, war stories still continued high on the list for movies. Hitlers Children was playing at the theatre that Darlene and I seriously contemplated attending. We were pondering our decision when two deep voices behind us said 'Hi', in unison.

We both turned around. Standing there were two sailors, both in navy blues. I immediately looked into the greenest pair of long lashed eyes. His smile was friendly and warm. Suddenly all thoughts of a movie vanished. He introduced himself as Jim

Carpenter…from Cleveland, Ohio. The other sailor, Don, seemed to favor talking to Darlene. As we stood beneath those flickering lights, I had no desire to share this part of Chicago with my new friend. I wanted Jim to see that place where my dreams were born. That part of Chicago that taught me how to continue those dreams. A street where neighbors laughed with one another, had block parties to get acquainted, and shared their hopes and desires with everyone.

St. John of God was having their annual August carnival. I asked Jim and Don if they would like to take a street car ride to the South side and visit the carnival. They thought the invitation perfect. As we sat together on that trolley ride to The Back of The Yards, Jim and I found out we had so much in common: We both came from a family that respected decency and worked diligently to keep their surroundings in livable order. Jim had a strict German catholic upbringing, although mine not as strict, I felt it most wonderful we were of the same religious faith.

That evening was without a doubt a dream in the making. I felt sure, before the evening even ended, this would be the man I would one day marry. I had little doubt that Fate brought him to me. She allowed me two more week-ends with Jim before he was shipped out to the Pacific. On that last day at the train station, Mama made sure Halina went along with me as a sort of chaperone. By now Mama probably guessed how strong my feelings were about this sailor. Without a doubt, as he kissed me good-bye that Saturday evening at the station, she had guessed correctly.

Only on Christmas Eve, when I drank too much wine, did I feel this heady. Never before had I felt such tingling in my legs. The butterflies in my stomach unceasingly fluttering. I was profoundly in love. Jim promised to write. I promised to answer. I now felt my future was secure.

Jim's letters came as often as the war allowed. With Paris liberated on August 25th, I felt sure the war was coming to an end. When the battle of the bulge began on December 16 and Glen Miller was killed on December 24th, I realized we still had a long way to go. I prayed ever harder for all the soldiers, especially for Jim.

January 1945 brought the joy of my senior year. Still working at Wrigley's, we received a box of gum at the end of every work week, which I promptly shipped out to Jim. It became a scarce commodity for everyone. In February I turned seventeen. My dreams and thoughts were those of Jim, marriage and a family. I wanted desperately to begin a life that would leave that mark of such dreams and memories I had. Jim's letters spoke of love and what he hoped our future together might bring...home, family and a happy life together. His values, his likes and dislikes were so like mine. I felt safe in what our future held.

March of 1945 took me to a job at Sears, Roebuck in the gift wrapping department. Music and words stirred my head and heart in a different ways now. You'll Never Know, I'll Be seeing You, Long Ago and Far Away, these were our songs now...Jim's and mine. They carried the words we wrote to one another. On April 1st, when the United States invaded Okinawa, the end of the war seemed close again. Sadly, President Roosevelt would not see that joyous day. He died of a cerebral hemorrhage on April 12th. Harry Truman became our president. Our nation and the world mourned the loss of a great president. The loss was trivial when Benito Mussolini and his mistress were killed and Hitler and his wife commited suicide.

Our prayers to the Blessed Mother were answered on May 8th when the war in Europe ended. When the atomic bomb was dropped on Hiroshima, Japan on August 6th, victory in Japan followed quickly on August 15th. The Nuremberg war crimes trials would forever act as a reminder of the evil of World war II brought into our world. Darlene was engaged to a sailor by the name of Bob Bell. Their marriage would take place immediately after our graduation in January of '46. Unfortunately the marriage would only last three years. She would eventually find happiness again, with a better man.

Joy reigned through our country and in my heart. My new found love was like a magic wand that lifted me from bed each morning. It was a feeling of joy and wonder. For the first time I knew what Mama must have felt like when she met Tata. I wanted to nurture this new feeling and have it grow strong and sturdy as my parents marriage and Tata's tree. That tree, a constant reminder what love can accomplish.

That autumn, as I walked through Sherman Park and on to the library, golden leaves crinkled beneath my feet, I gave God thanks that the war had ended. I was still sending packages of gum and cookies to various service men, and most of all to that one that now held a special place in my heart. Mama was feeling somewhat better, probably more because my Aunt and Uncle were at last returning to Chicago.

As a senior I was offered the opportunity to work part time at the job that would become my full time position after graduation. Working at Chicago Title and Trust threw me fully into the working business world. Darlene kept in touch, albeit sporadically now, because of her engagement and upcoming marriage. Moving to another city after her marriage, we lost touch. Only after her divorce did I see her once or twice. She remarried a few years later and moved to California.

When graduation arrived in January of 1946, it suddenly seemed the years had gone by too quickly. Commencement was held at Northwest University. Mama and Tata attended this final day of my schooling with great pride in their eyes. I thought my education was finally over. It was only the beginning.

That spring Mr. Kremls flowers seemed gloriously brighter to me then ever. The lilac bush in Miss Slatky's yard looked fuller and smelled much sweeter. It seemed like only yesterday Rosemary and I stopped to buy our penny candy at this grocery store after a morning of roller skating.

Did it seem like only yesterday that I was so small I could only watch as Tata or Mama watered the maple tree? And only yesterday that I pulled out that hose to water down the sidewalk, then lifting the hose higher to spray every leaf on Tata's tree. The droplets of water on each leaf swimming about like sparkling diamonds in the morning sun.

Warm evenings still echoed the sounds of neighbors sitting outdoors, laughing and talking while children shouted delight in a game of hide and seek. This spring I sat on the green bench and dreamed of Jim's homecoming. Trying to read a book, hardly knowing what I was reading. I could only hope that one day my own children would know and enjoy what Tata and Mama envisioned and brought to this street called Loomis.

Halina was in high school now and enjoying her days of youth to the fullest. We still had our moments of closeness, when we talked or attended a movie. May would bring many changes…Jim's return, our engagement and our eventual marriage in December. I would nurture and love every moment of my new life with him. Jim talked of settling down in Cleveland. The way I felt I knew I would follow him to the ends of the world. Yet I felt sad in the knowledge that my life on Loomis might be coming to an end. Babsha felt sadness when she moved to this country. So did Tata and Mama when their world suddenly changed. Just as they did, I would survive any change. Like Tata's tree, I would continue to grow and stay strong.

ABOUT THE AUTHOR

Pat Carpenter-Wood, born in 1928, was raised in the Back of the Yards. Although she now resides in Tucson, Arizona, she has never forgotten the roots that still lay deep on Chicago's south side or her Polish heritage.

She attended Hamline Grammar School, Gage Park High School, and Jones Commercial School. She greets each day, just as her parents did so many years ago, with faith and hope in new beginnings.

At 72, she is planning to continue her writing career. She is now working on a new story that deals with emotional abuse, titled 'Blue Heaven'. She would also appreciate any input from readers of 'Tata's Tree'. All comments will be treasured.

Her e-mail address is: patcwdnetzero.net.